# SOUNDS OF FREEDOM

# SOUNDS OF FREEDOM

## MUSICIANS ON SPIRITUALITY & SOCIAL CHANGE

John Malkin

PARALLAX PRESS

BERKELEY, CALIFORNIA

Parallax Press
P.O. Box 7355
Berkeley, CA 94707
www.parallax.org

Parallax Press is the publishing division of Unified Buddhist Church, Inc.

Cover and text design by Gopa & Ted 2, Inc.

Photo Credits: Laurie Anderson by Maggie Soladay; Ani DiFranco by Danny Clinch;
Michael Franti by anonymous; Indigo Girls by Frank W. Ockenfels; Rickie Lee Jones
by Gregg Segal; Tom Morello by Danny Clinch; Holly Near by Mike Rogers;
Utah Phillips, photo provided; Steve Reich by Wonge Bergmann; Boots Riley
by Victor Hall; Michelle Shocked by Nurha de Souza; John Trudell by Ronnie
Farley; Goapele Mohlabane by Robin Twomey; Philip Glass by Stewart Cohen;
Darryl Cherney by Greg King; John Malkin by Caroline Nicola.

Thich Nhat Hanh's Introduction is an edited transcript of a talk given June 8, 2004.

Library of Congress Cataloging-in-Publication Data

Sounds of freedom : musicians on spirituality & social change /
edited by John Malkin.
p. cm.
ISBN 1-888375-47-7 (pbk.)
1. Music—Social aspects. 2. Spirituality in music. 3.
Musicians—Interviews. I. Malkin, John.

ML3916.S68 2005
780'.03—dc22
2005003467

1  2  3  4  5 / 09  08  07  06  05

For my paternal grandparents, Jennie and John Malkin.
Their compassion, generosity, and dedication to helping others
have inspired me to reach for peace, freedom, and justice.

# TABLE OF CONTENTS

# FOREWORD: THE DREAM

THICH NHAT HANH

SOME TIME AGO I had a dream that I was a music student. In my dream, I learned that I had been accepted into a class taught by the best teacher at the university. It was an honor to be a student in his class, and I told my friends about my acceptance. One of them was also a student, but she had not been accepted into the class. She was very kind and said, "Never mind, you are accepted, it's just like I am accepted."

The first day of class, I had to walk through many doors. There were a lot of students, and the class was at the top of the building. Suddenly, I saw a young man trying to make his way into a room. The young student looked exactly like me; he was my mirror image. I was very surprised to see me outside of myself. How could he be me? I went to the office nearby and asked the lady in charge of registration, "Who is he? Has he been accepted into that class too?" She said, "No, he has not."

Only after I woke up did I understand the meaning of the first part of this dream. Tripitaka Master Hsuan-tsang of China lived in the Tang dynasty. He went to India in search of Buddhist scriptures and he wanted to go to the Gridhrakuta Mountain where the Buddha resided, to ask the Buddha for the scriptures—the direct way! He and three of his students set out for the mountain, but they needed to cross a very large river. There was only one boat on the shore and the boat had no bottom. The boatman said, "Well, this river has only one ferry boat, and this is it. If you want to use it, the opportunity is there. If you are afraid, then you'll stay on this shore forever." All of them were very eager to get the scriptures and to meet the Buddha, so they ventured down and sat in the boat.

They began crossing the river and yet they did not drown. When they had gone halfway across, Tripitaka Master Hsuan-tsang saw the body of a drowned man floating on the river. He asked the boatman, "Who is that person? Whose corpse is that?" The boatman looked at him intensely and said, "You don't know? It's you. You have shed that body by having the courage to step on this boat. You have released that mundane, secular body and you have got a holy body. That's you. If you do not die, there's no way for you to cross the river as a new being." When I woke up I remembered all the details of that story, and I began to understand that if I had not died as that student, I could not have been accepted into that teacher's class. I had to let go of my self, my ego that wanted to be in the class, before I could go in.

In the second part of the dream, I was still trying to get to class. In order to get to the class, I had to go through many corridors, some of them dark. At one point I walked through a hall filled with musical instruments. I knew I was supposed to take one and then go to the class, but I did not. Finally I reached the classroom. When I opened the door, I saw that the room was huge. I had thought there would be twenty or twenty-five people, but there were several thousand of them sitting and waiting for the teacher to arrive. Looking out, I saw stars, suns, moons, peaks of mountains covered with snow, cascades, and waterfalls. I had the impression that I had been there before. The scenery was so familiar. It was our true home, the place we want to come and to be all of our life—all the wonders of life, a highly spiritual kind of landscape. I felt very at home. This was my place.

As usual, I didn't want to sit in the middle. I found a corner where I could sit quietly and observe. But someone came up to me and said: "Today it's your turn to make a presentation; you have to move to the center." "What presentation?"—I was not prepared to make a presentation to this huge class and this illustrious teacher. But I had to go. And I was thinking: what kind of thing am I going to do? Out of habit, I put my hand into my pocket and took out something very small. It was a miniature bell.

Suddenly I got enlightenment, I had great confidence, and I realized that with this mini-bell I could play music—because I know how to invite the bell, that's true. This music is wonderful, because it brings harmony, calm, peace, and enlightenment to you and to the whole community. I had been practicing listening to the bell and inviting the bell all my life, and I had not realized that I was practicing music—the kind of spiritual music that brings peace, harmony, mutual understanding, and happiness to people. So with that small bell, I had great confidence that I would please the teacher and the assembly. And with that I woke up.

I am convinced that each of us has a bell in our pockets. We can be students of music. We can help bring harmony and peace and joy into our bodies and our minds. And we have not just one, but many musical instruments. Our in-breath and out-breath is a kind of violin that we can play all day. Our steps, our lungs, our noses—everything can become a musical instrument. We can play music while sitting, while walking, or while eating—and that music will bring joy, calm, and peace into our lives. And as I am a student of that class, I invite all of you to be my co-students, and you will learn how to play music in such a way that will bring peace to our society, our communities, and ourselves.

# SOUNDS OF FREEDOM

# INTRODUCTION:
# A NEW AMERICAN REVOLUTION

JOHN MALKIN

WE ARE LIVING in a time of great unrest and change. People in the world are struggling to reduce poverty, exploitation, and suffering. We are living in a time of violence but also in a time of great awakening. We are creating a new American revolution connected to a global movement for peace and justice. In this continuously unfolding revolution, we see the possibility of living free from anger and fear. We can imagine creating personal and international relationships firmly rooted in self-determination, cooperation, and equality.

Every movement needs music. The sixteen musicians in *Sounds of Freedom* are contributing a soundtrack for this new American revolution. In this book and the accompanying CD, they speak with open hearts about their relationship to social change and spiritual growth. Many speak for the first time about how their own spiritual and political understanding has affected them as artists and activists. These personal discussions were originally broadcast on the Great Leap Forward, a radio program I produced for the underground radio station, Free Radio Santa Cruz. For eight years, the program has provided a home for music, spirituality, and activism.

The human experiment in ending violence with violence has proven unsuccessful. The artists within these pages offer alternative strategies for cultivating empowerment and for alleviating the economic, environmental, and social suffering of our times. They shine as great examples of how music, personal insight, and social activism can be integrated as a potent antidote to war, commercialism, and the propaganda of fear. They are remarkable innovators in this contemporary revolution of the spirit, and they are not alone.

These musicians follow in the footsteps of Paul Robeson, Billie Holiday, Bob Marley, Pete Seeger and the Weavers, Janis Joplin, Sweet Honey in the Rock, and hundreds of other musicians who have challenged injustice and used their music to both inspire and accompany social change. Some of those groundbreakers are still leading the way today; others have passed on. Still others, brilliant and needed voices, did not make it into this book but will make it into the next. This book is just one mighty gathering of many.

One role of the artist in our society is to act as a warning signal—to alert the wider community to signs of danger to personal and collective freedom, health, and well-being. These artists do that and more—they point directly to paths of freedom and peace. Many of them have performed and spoken out at protests against a string of U.S. wars—in Vietnam, Central America, Panama, Afghanistan, and Iraq. They have inspired generations of music fans to take action in myriad social change realms including gay and lesbian rights, environmental protection, human and civil rights, indigenous peoples' autonomy, freedom for Tibet, and the release of political prisoners such as Geronimo Pratt, Mumia Abu-Jamal, and Leonard Peltier. In recent years, they have entertained and invigorated critical masses of activists at global corporatization protests in Seattle, Genoa, Cancún, and elsewhere. They have established organizations—such as Rage Against the Machine's Axis of Justice and Rickie Lee Jones' Furniture for the People—to inform their fans and help them connect with opportunities for activism.

Some of the musicians in *Sounds of Freedom* have been involved in national organizations such as Earth First! (Darryl Cherney), the American Indian Movement (John Trudell), and Honor the Earth (Indigo Girls). Ani DiFranco and others recently led efforts among rock 'n' roll musicians to encourage fans to be politically active and participate in the 2004 U.S. presidential elections.

Of course, no two of us imagine freedom exactly the same way, and these musicians express a variety of sounds and poetics, drawing from such musical traditions as classical, jazz, punk, hip hop, folk, and electronic. In the African- and Asian-inspired polyrhythms of Steve Reich's pulsing and phasing compositions and the Native American chants, instrumentation, and philosophy of John Trudell's rock-infused compositions, we hear a taste of true world music. Boots Riley, Indigo Girls, and Goapele give us musical poems that connect us with our own feelings and the joys and sorrows of others.

There is the jazz-infused voice of Rickie Lee Jones, the guitar mastery of Tom Morello, the musical diversity of Michelle Shocked, and the compassionate call for change of Michael Franti. With their innovative understandings of music, Laurie Anderson and Philip Glass have created new categories unto themselves. Holly Near, Utah Phillips, Darryl Cherney, and Ani DiFranco bring three very different sensibilities to the art of folk music and storytelling. These artists are also influenced by diverse spiritual traditions, from Judaism, Christianity, and Buddhism to atheism and paganism. Their common ground is their commitment to creativity and their openness in exploring truth and freedom.

Through words and music these artists explore political, social, and spiritual consciousness and synthesize new understandings. They take risks and challenge the dominant consciousness and record industry status quo. As popular artists living in the United States in the twenty-first century, these musicians have taken on a critical role. Though the U.S. government is now considered the lone superpower on Earth, it is facing a formidable opponent in the form of world opinion. The global movement for peace has called for an end to war, poverty, exploitation, racism, and environmental destruction. The musicians in *Sounds of Freedom* are helping build this new revolution and giving it a beat. We can all dance into this new world together.

May this book alleviate suffering and help all beings to be peaceful, happy, and free.

# STRIVING FOR BALANCE

AN INTERVIEW WITH ANI DIFRANCO

more and more there is this animal looking out through my eyes
at all the traffic on the road to nowhere
at all the shiny stuff around to buy, at all the wires in the air
at all the people shopping for the same blank stare
at america the drastic, that isolated geographic
that's become infested with millionaires
—from "Animal" by Ani DiFranco

ANI DIFRANCO is a prolific songwriter, singer, and musician known for her strong lyrics, percussive guitar style, and highly energized live shows. Her work spans many musical genres, from folk-punk to jazz-funk, illuminating and celebrating our humanness.

Born in Buffalo, New York in 1970, DiFranco started performing in local bars at the age of nine. She moved out of her mother's apartment at the age of fifteen and began writing her own material and performing regularly at the Essex Street Pub. She graduated from the Visual and Performing Arts High School at sixteen and played all of Buffalo's clubs many times before moving to New York City.

In 1990, when she was nineteen years old, DiFranco formed her own independent record company, Righteous Babe Records, and released her first album, *Ani DiFranco*. Since then, her label has released more than twenty albums by DiFranco as well as albums by other artists including Sara Lee, Dan Bern, and Arto Lindsey.

To help her own community, DiFranco contracts with other locally owned Buffalo companies to print and manufacture all Righteous Babe products. She uses independent record distributors in the U.S., Canada, and Europe, and is refurbishing historic buildings in Buffalo, including a long-neglected church that was recently transformed into the new office of Righteous Babe Records.

DiFranco's is a music of integrity and authenticity, made to challenge the status quo. Her work, which blends a punk DIY (do-it-yourself) ethic with sensuous and playful lyrics, exhibits a tireless struggle against the commodification and homogenization of music. It also highlights her opposition to militarism and the death penalty, and her support of queer visibility and feminist issues, including women's reproductive rights.

DiFranco also appeared on the 2004 CD, *For the Lady*. It was compiled to benefit the U.S. Campaign for Burma and to support freedom for 1991 Nobel Peace Prize recipient Aung San Suu Kyi, who had participated in the 1988 nonviolent democratic uprising in Burma and was arrested for her calls for democracy and freedom. In July 2004, DiFranco and fellow artist Damien Rice became the first American musicians to visit refugee camps in Burma and Thailand and meet with pro-democracy activists in the region. They visited a "safe house" in Thailand where former political prisoners passed a guitar around, sharing songs with DiFranco.

DiFranco tours worldwide much of the year. But she spent the period leading up to the 2004 presidential election in U.S. swing states on her Vote Dammit! Tour, where she led the move by rock 'n' roll musicians to encourage their fans to participate in the political process. Ohio congressman and presidential candidate Dennis Kucinich joined DiFranco on the tour, which also featured a slide show on the history of voting in the United States.

In the liner notes of her Grammy-nominated CD *Educated Guess*, DiFranco writes, "How can one talk on the role of politics in art when art is activism and anyway both are just a lifelong light shining through a swinging prism?" Her latest album, *Knuckledown*, features a song titled "Paradigm" that paints a picture of her mother's activism, a major influence in DiFranco's drive for activism and democracy:

> i was born to two immigrants who knew why they were here
> they were happy to pay taxes
> for the schools and roads
> happy to be here
> they took it seriously
> the second job of citizenry

my mother went campaigning door to door
just a girl in a room full of women
licking stamps and laughing
i remember the feeling of community brewing
of democracy happening.

DiFranco is an uncompromising artist and activist, seeking truth and an equilibrium with paradox. On her website she lays out her personal philosophy about freedom: "I speak without reservation from what I know and who I am. I do so with the understanding that all people should have the right to offer their voice to the chorus, whether the result is harmony or dissonance."

▼ ▼ ▼ ▼ ▼

**John Malkin:** You were very active before the November 2004 election in get-out-the-vote efforts. What is it about the current state of the world that makes you feel so strongly about encouraging your fans to be politically active and vote? What is at stake?

**Ani DiFranco:** In every desperate situation, such as the political circumstances we find ourselves in these days, we have great opportunities for change, dialogue. I guess it is about trying to be smart and strategic and capitalize on that opportunity.

A whole lot of people in this country are becoming aware that we haven't been participating as citizens. Voting participation is really low, especially among young people. I'm interested in using this crisis as an opportunity to get people inspired to participate once again. It would be great if people registered and voted in every election from now on. It would be a lifestyle shift in this country, from consumers back to citizens.

**JM:** What kind of response did you get from audiences during the Vote Dammit! tour?

**AD:** It was quite thrilling. Tons of people registered to vote at the shows in the swing states. I was sharing the stage with other political artists including

Dan Bern, Margaret Cho, Indigo Girls, and Suzanne Westenhoefer. It felt like the atmosphere of inspiration was pretty high everywhere we went.

JM: One popular view of rock 'n' roll—particularly punk rock—is that it lives outside of politics and even that fans are apathetic about social change. Do you think that holds true anymore, if it ever did?

AD: Talking about apathy or engagement in rock 'n' roll is like talking about "what women want"! I think for every little cultural scene that springs up here and there, with each direction in rock or pop music, or for every artist within that, there is a different degree of engagement or apathy. I am a hopeful creature, and it feels to me like young people are coming out from under the sort of corporate-consumerist mind-control of the mass media and beginning to support and design political art and build a resistance culturally as well as politically. It seems to me that people are making more room for political music these days. I think that it is probably a cyclical thing, like everything.

JM: You mention your hopefulness. How do you keep grounded these days amid the war and deception? How do you cultivate hope in yourself?

AD: At the same time that all of those horrible, destructive things are happening there are also amazing things happening. Political art is out there, whether it is supported in the mainstream culture or not. More and more I try to focus my energies and attention on the people who are doing the good work, who are out there being active and creative and designing alternatives. Working with them is incredibly life affirming, inspiring, and hopeful.

Sometimes I show up to venues in cities and people shout out things like, "Talk about George Bush, Ani!" I say, "No! What, are you kidding me? [laughter] You can turn on any TV station and hear all about him!" I want to talk about all the people the major media is ignoring. Our heroes are the people who are out there to inspire and empower. It keeps me hopeful to dedicate my own energy to helping people who are doing great things.

JM: This brings to mind "Grand Canyon," a song on *Educated Guess*. You sing on it, "i love my country, by which i mean i am indebted joyfully to all of the people throughout its history who have fought the government to make right." Are there people who have particularly inspired you?

AD: There are so many! We have such a long and glorious activist history. In this atmosphere of shame and helplessness and anger and complete disillusionment with the political apparatus, I wanted a tool to build hope from the stage. So I wrote "Grand Canyon" as a patriotic poem. My patriotism is of a democratic variety, as opposed to the fascist version of patriot being put forth by the media and the administration. Their vision of a patriot is of a blindly accepting, non-questioning drone. But Mark Twain stated it really well: "Loyalty to the country always, loyalty to the government when it deserves it." My patriotism is born of the cultural and activist history of my country. The land, the beautiful land that we inhabit, everything we hold dear about this country, all of the rights and freedoms that we brag about around the world, were fought for by activists. None of them were granted benevolently by power. From the original revolutionaries who overthrew the king, right up to today, and all of the political struggles that citizens are undertaking for justice and for freedom and peace. That is what that poem is about.

JM: What is your experience with integrating the personal and the political, social change and spiritual growth?

AD: That is a very deep, important question in this twenty-first century. The political movements that I know of, the left of my time and place, seem to be in opposition to spiritual modalities. I understand this because many of our religious systems are extremely patriarchal and, I know for myself, quickly lose appeal for that very reason! Certainly women can and have and will continue to find their own place within traditional religions. But I think [our place is] in our political systems as well as our spiritual ones. Then, I think, we can find a modern coming together of spirituality and activism.

I believe you need both. It cannot be a choice for people. Our struggle for society, for community, for all humanity, must be at one with our struggle to become ourselves. I think that a really powerful political movement has a spiritual center to it. But I think we also need a new spirituality that is as evolved as our global resistance. If you look around the world, all stories, as they go from bad to worse, have patriarchy as a common denominator. I long for a spiritual core to a progressive movement that is uplifting for all of us.

JM: In the song "Origami", you sing, "men are delicate origami creatures who need women to unfold them." This song seems to relate to the present state of our world. Men are generally at the helm of political and economic institutions and have created a world struggling with poverty, hunger, and permanent warfare. What are your thoughts about that?

AD: In addition to speaking about my personal experience, that song also speaks to the paradox in all of us. Men, as we know, are supposed to be strong. When I first started playing that song on stage, it made the audience laugh. As soon as I said that line "men are delicate…" the audience had some kind of nervous reaction, as if it were a bit of a shock.

I think that the masculine and the feminine are contained within each of us and when I talk about a desire to shift from patriarchy to a balance of power, it is much more complicated than saying just that women should step into all of those offices. I'm talking about a different way of thinking. There is a masculine and a feminine intention in each of us. Our religious and political culture lacks an understanding of paradox. There is this oversimplification that becomes "good and evil," "right and wrong," and "us and them." Maybe my song can challenge these basic ways of thinking in some way. My little folksongs never want to miss a challenge along the way!

JM: One strategy for social change believes that we can seize power and transform it and then hand it back to the people. It sounds like you are talking about changing one's point of view.

AD: Yes, I could dig myself a really deep philosophical hole. I am on a journey to understand the pervasiveness of patriarchy in all of the world and in myself. It is a hard thing to verbalize, but I tried to articulate it in the song "Evolve":

cuz they are locking our sons and our daughters in cages
they are taking by the thousands
our lives from under us

it's a crash course in religious fundamentals
now let's all go to war
get some bang for our buck.

I am becoming transfixed by nature and my part in it. I have made this journey for myself, to look at the time before all of the patriarchal religions began, and discovered a spirituality for myself that is based in nature. I think that all moral lessons can be found in nature before they are interpreted through human culture. Peace, for example, is a product of balance. An ecosystem will teach us this. When there is turmoil and change and chaos in the universe, then there is pain and destruction. But when there is a balance, we achieve peace. This idea can be applied to economies, governments, and people within a society. Violence begets violence. Aggression begets aggression. It is a natural law.

Historically, women's modes of spirituality have been more connected with nature, and therefore marginalized and ostracized by patriarchal religious structures. I think that we need to, in our journey to incorporate the feminine, understand ourselves as animals, as parts of an ecosystem, and as beholden to that first and foremost.

JM: On one of the three albums you released in 1999, *To the Teeth*, you sing,

we are armed to the teeth
we are all working together now
to make our lives mercifully brief.

Can you expand a little bit on how you feel about nonviolence? How important is that to you in creating social change?

AD: As an animal, I acknowledge the existence of violence. That sounds a little goofy, doesn't it? I eat meat, for instance. But I do so in moderation. I don't feel that it is shameful to be a carnivore, but I do feel that the meat industry's abuse of animals is shameful. I don't want to promote or support that whole system of animal cruelty, but vegetarianism is not black and white for me. It is the same thing with violence. It is also part of our nature. It is a part of nature. But, again, there has to be balance. We can handle a certain amount of violence. We can handle a certain amount of pollution in our bodies. We can have a drink now and then. But too much and we are out of balance and we are sick and we are gone.

I think that our culture is very sick. Rather than striving for perfection or slipping into absolute passivity, I think we need to strive for balance.

JM: How does balance play out in your music making and album producing? You have said that self-loathing and insecurity are an inherent part of the process of producing an album, as are bravery and confidence.

AD: Once again, it's a paradox. When I am making an album, at times I think, Oh my God, I hate myself! This is dumb, this album is all wrong. I can't release it. But then I just keep moving, and it turns out fine. I am my own best critic, and that propels me and also debilitates me. Like any one of our character traits as people, our greatest strengths are often our undoing as well. Does that answer the question?

JM: I guess there is a deeper question here about this country. Though the United States is so plentiful in resources and wealth, a lot of people are very unhappy. I am curious what your thoughts are. There is a story about when the Dalai Lama first came to the United States to give public talks and answer questions. He was quite surprised to hear Americans asking about how to deal with self-hatred. It apparently was not a question that had been posed by people in Asia and India.

AD: Interesting. I think that's a big part of capitalist marketing. Hyperconsumerism pulls people away from empowerment and into a place where we believe that if we have just the right hair and the right car and are thin enough, then we'll be happy. These are very isolating, very individualist, and very self-denigrating ways of thinking. Empowerment and community and being active and connected with other people is really the path to joy and understanding of yourself as a beautiful and worthy being just as you are.

One of the things that helps me most in making art, what carries me through, is often just the feeling that I don't want the most beautiful or perfect record—I just want an honest expression. In art, I don't want to do what always works. I want to explore. I want to be intrepid, and that means failure.

That means that not everything is successful. But success isn't what I look for in art. I look for things that are compelling or challenging. I want to find my own aspirations and crawl out from under this image that is marketed to us of what we are supposed to be.

JM: In your poem "Literal" you point to Jesus and Christianity and the danger that comes from attachment to ideas. I hear you pointing out that truth and poetry can sometimes be squeezed out of messages of original compassion and justice. And that that leaves behind sort of a fundamentalist dogma. Tell me more about that.

AD: This poem is about the dangers of literal thinking. As a writer, I tend to think non-literally and more metaphorically. Another lesson I've learned from nature is that everything is connected to everything else. You look at cotton plants and there are clouds in there. You look at cracks in mud and there's the skin of your hand. Everything is analogous to everything else.

I think the way we interpret nature and our world is essential. With the spiritual doctrines we live with, such as the Bible, I think a poetic interpretation is always more real than a literal one. To look at words on a paper and try to interpret them as literally as possible, ignoring the fact that they were written there by somebody who was already interpreting the truth, can be very destructive and lead to a real absence of spirituality. Really you have—well, what do you have then? A mess! [Laughter]

I am becoming less and less wedded to absolutes. Truth is very contextual. To understand the specificity of your own life is so important. My believing in freedom of choice for women to determine the fate of their own bodies and control their own reproductive systems is part of this feeling. What is right for me is not necessarily right for you. Because we have completely different lives, maybe. We are born of very different circumstances, so different truths apply. Absolute black-and-white, good-and-evil, literal thinking is contradictory to that fluidity of truth.

JM: Do you think that openness to interpretation and leaving behind absolutism brings freedom?

AD: I think it just brings a healthier complexity. I don't think matriarchy is the answer to patriarchy. There needs to be balance. Of course, we need certain laws that apply to all of us, such as "Thou shalt not kill." We need to hang on to things like that, a certain sort of absolute. But even that law has contextual exceptions. There is a highly evolved tradition of trying to make the collective ensure the rights of the individual, and I think that is a glorious concept. And then there is the other need to ensure that each individual promotes the good of the collective. Both pursuits are necessary. Between them resonates a balance and an energy that will bring peace.

**JM:** Finally, what do you think is the importance now of independent media?

**AD:** Its importance is greater than ever! We need to put into action Abbie Hoffman's suggestion: "Don't hate the media, become the media!"

These days when we talk about presidential races or big "P" Politics, we tend to get sucked into this cult of personality that is all around us. We're taught to think of politics as a contest between these two dudes. "Which one looks cuter in a flight suit? Which one has a better smile? We'll vote for him!" The truth of course is that these men are not kings. They are heads of huge political parties. Changing the president could mean a whole new administration of people and thousands of judicial appointments that could include more progressive people. The ripple effect would be huge, and includes, for example, the independent renegade radio stations being able to broadcast their art and their ideas without having the FCC come and rip down their antenna. This is the kind of change in atmosphere that we need. Imagine if we had a whole country full of good human beings who are somewhat out of crisis mode and who could begin to increase the momentum of their good work.

# Ani DiFranco Selected Discography

*Ani DiFranco* – 1990 (Righteous Babe Records)

*Not So Soft* – 1991 (Righteous Babe Records)

*Imperfectly* – 1992 (Righteous Babe Records)

*Puddle Dive* – 1993 (Righteous Babe Records)

*Like I Said* – 1993 (Righteous Babe Records)

*Out of Range* – 1994 (Righteous Babe Records)

*Not A Pretty Girl* – 1995 (Righteous Babe Records)

*Dilate* – 1996 (Righteous Babe Records)

*The Past Didn't Go Anywhere* with Utah Phillips – 1996 (Righteous
  Babe Records)

*More Joy, Less Shame* – 1996 (Righteous Babe Records)

*Living In A Clip* – 1997 (Righteous Babe Records)

*Little Plastic Castle* – 1998 (Righteous Babe Records)

*Up Up Up Up Up Up* – 1999 (Righteous Babe Records)

*Little Plastic Remixes* – 1999 (Righteous Babe Records)

*Fellow Workers* – 1999 (Righteous Babe Records)

*Prize* – 1999 (Righteous Babe Records)

*To The Teeth* – 1999 (Righteous Babe Records)

*Swing Set* – 2000 (Righteous Babe Records)

*Til We Outnumber 'Em* Compilation Album – 2000 (Righteous Babe Records)

*Revelling Reckoning* – 2001 (Righteous Babe Records)

*Render* – 2002 (Righteous Babe Records)

*So Much Shouting, So Much Laughter* – 2002 (Righteous Babe Records)

*Evolve* – 2003 (Righteous Babe Records)

*Peace Not War* Compilation Album – 2003

*Educated Guess* – 2004 (Righteous Babe Records)

*Trust* – 2004 (Righteous Babe Records)

*KnuckleDown* – 2005 (Righteous Babe Records)

# POWER TO THE PEACEFUL

AN INTERVIEW WITH MICHAEL FRANTI

Every single soul is a poem
Written on the back of God's hand.
—from "Every Single Soul" by Michael Franti

IN AUGUST OF 2000, thousands of people gathered in Los Angeles to protest the "politics as usual" at the Democratic National Convention. The event drew people of all colors, ages, and walks of life, each with his or her own cause and reason for being there. It had been a long, hot day and most people seemed exhausted. Then Michael Franti and Spearhead started singing, "all the freaky people make the beauty of the world." The crowd started dancing. Soon, the words became the reality; a tired mass of individuals revealed themselves as a smiling, energized community committed to social change.

Michael Franti was born on April 21, 1968. He was adopted and raised by white parents in a predominantly black neighborhood in Oakland, California. He found his birth parents at the age of twenty-two, after searching for them for two years. He learned that his birth parents, a white mother and black father, had chosen not to raise him because they feared racist repercussions. He would later write a song about his childhood experience titled, "Socio-Genetic Experience." Franti is now the father of two sons.

In 1986, he formed the band The Beatnigs with Rono Tse. They released one self-titled album on Jello Biafra's Alternative Tentacles record label. The album brought together elements of industrial, punk, and hip hop music and featured politically conscious songs.

In 1990, he created a new band called the Disposable Heroes of Hiphoprisy, with Rono Tse and guitarist Charlie Hunter. Their debut album, *Hipho-*

*prisy Is the Greatest Luxury* was released in 1992 and included the songs "Music and Politics" and "Television: Drug of the Nation." The Disposable Heroes of Hiphoprisy opened shows for an eclectic range of bands, including Public Enemy, Nirvana, Arrested Development, and U2. Rono Tse went on to work with the Bay Area rap band Mystic Journeymen, and Charlie Hunter formed his own popular jazz trio, the Charlie Hunter Trio. Franti formed Spearhead.

Spearhead's 1994 debut album, *Home*, was released by Capitol Records. The soulful sound and insightful lyrics brought the songwriter new attention. On each new album Franti and his band have addressed political and social issues with a growing sensitivity and compassion. Of *Stay Human* (2001), Franti has written, " 'Stay human' is an expression that I began using a while back to combat what I have seen as a growing attack on the souls of loving individuals on this sweet, sweet planet of ours...it is my belief that we are spiritual beings learning to live in a human form, not the other way around....Through music we can reconnect, mind, body and spirit."

Franti started his own record label, Boo Boo Wax in 2000 "to further divorce ourselves from corporate tyranny." Releases on the new label have included *Michael Franti: Live at the Baobab*, and *Songs from the Front Porch* (2003).

The transformation of Michael Franti's music over time has been accompanied by a simultaneous deepening of his own social activism and personal growth. He continues to offer a clear criticism of oppressive and totalitarian institutions based in a compassionate understanding that all people want to live free from fear and war and in joyful and cooperative communities. As the title song from his latest album states:

> Everyone deserves music
> Even your worst enemies deserve music.

In 1999, Franti organized the first 911 Power to the Peaceful Festival, which now attracts up to 20,000 people annually. Held in Golden Gate Park in San Francisco, the 911 festival is an international day of art, activism, and music. In 2001, Franti took time out during a European tour to visit a former World War II concentration camp near Hamburg, Germany. In June 2004, he traveled to Israel, Palestine, and Iraq to speak to people about their life and the war. During his Middle East trip, he played guitar for children in hospitals who had been wounded during U.S. bombings, for people who invited him into their homes, for off-duty soldiers in their bar and for on-duty soldiers on the street who just wanted to hear a song for a moment. In Iraq, people asked him to pose this question to people back in the United States: "How would you feel if the Iraqi government came over here, overthrew the government and occupied your country?"

I met Michael Franti at his studio and office in the Mission district of San Francisco. We both sat cross-legged and barefoot on a couch in the lobby. Franti hasn't worn shoes since August 2004, when he initiated a three-day shoe fast. (He wears shoes only on airplanes and in restaurants). The renunciation of footwear began as an experiment to enhance his awareness and understanding of the poverty that much of the world struggles with everyday. It also inspired the lyrics for one of my favorite Spearhead songs:

> If I could be you and you could be me
> I could walk a mile in your shoes
> And you could walk a mile in my bare feet.

▼ ▼ ▼ ▼ ▼

**John Malkin**: On your latest album, *Everyone Deserves Music*, you sing, "We can bomb the world to pieces, but we can't bomb it into peace." What is your view on the effectiveness of violence and nonviolence for creating the world we want?

**Michael Franti**: The phrase, "We can bomb the world to pieces, but we can't bomb it into peace," came to me when we were doing a Power to the Peaceful festival. The festival began five years ago as the concert for Mumia Abu-Jamal, the imprisoned death row activist. Mumia was appealing his death penalty conviction and to draw attention to the emergency status of Mumia's case, we selected September 11, 9-1-1, because of the emergency number that we dial. After September 11, 2001, obviously, that day got a new significance. We decided to put on a peace concert. We had a meeting before the show and Pam Africa was speaking and she said something that was almost like "We can bomb the world to pieces, but we can't bomb it to peace," but she said it over about ten sentences. I just condensed it into one phrase.

Ever since September 11, our nation has been feeling a lot of pain, a lot of hurt, a lot of anger, a lot of frustration, and a lot of fear. People are questioning the future. When you are in that much of a state of emotional chaos, it is easy to follow somebody who says, "I have a way for you to ease your pain. We are going to go after these people who did this horrible thing and we are going to take them out. Then you won't have to think or worry or fear it anymore." That's a very simplistic view that the Bush administration has put out not only to us, but to the rest of the world. This government has imposed the ultimatum: "You are either with us in this view or you are with the terrorists."

I don't hold that view and I don't hold the view that bombing buildings and select targets is going to bring us any closer to peace, either. I believe that all bombing is terrorism, no matter who is doing it. We need to begin to look at the reasons behind these violent acts, to be able to deescalate and find resolution. The targets for September 11 were not chosen arbitrarily. This was a calculated and deliberate choice.

The World Trade Center is the center for corporate control, the Pentagon is the center for military control, and the White House is the home of our foreign policies. Maybe we should begin to look at those three areas and the effects they have on the rest of the world. Creating more war-torn areas in Afghanistan and Iraq has not brought us more peace and stability. For every bullet that has been fired, every bomb dropped, and every leader overthrown, we've just created one more child who grows up thinking that militaristic solutions are the way to get things done on this planet.

JM: People often feel that they must choose between social change or spiritual growth. That we need to work on addressing our own suffering or the suffering of the world around us. But a lot of people have done both. Martin Luther King, Jr. and Gandhi are good examples of that. The Dalai Lama recently spoke about the importance of love and compassion and forgiveness in social change. He said that religion and politics need to go together. What is your view on this?

MF: Well, I was in a yoga class last night and the last thing my teacher said before we left the class was, "You practice yoga on your mat and you live yoga in your life." There are many definitions for yoga but one that I particularly resonate with is that yoga means union with the creative force of life. The exercising part may or may not bring us closer to union with God, but it is a way that we can begin to connect with this spiritual force. But we can also practice that union with the divine in other parts of our life. Our daily actions either lead us towards union or separate us from it. We either come closer to love and kindness and compassion or we move further away. With every action—the way that we spend our money, the way that we treat one another when we walk down the street, the way that we raise our children, the way that we look at the outside world—we can ask ourselves if we are helping to promote goodness and well-being for all beings on the planet.

I don't think it is a question of whether or not we should combine our spirituality with our activism because our spirituality is with us no matter what we do. Wherever we go. The question is, how can we continue to feed our souls and work at the pace and with the centeredness of love that we want to work and make social change. It is not hard to become an activist. All you've got to do is show up. And it is not even hard to show up two or three times. But it is hard to show up for two or three years. Or two or three decades. Or two or three lifetimes.

Spirituality is that thing that keeps us from going crazy. It gives us the determination and that centeredness of love in our heart to continue to move on, and it inspires us, and that is the reason that I make music. I want to inspire other people to say, "Hey, yeah, this world is a place that is still worth loving for and directing our actions for in a positive way. It is not a place that we have to give up on yet."

JM: You went to Seattle in 1999 for the protests against the World Trade Organization and you have been involved in the protests against all of the recent wars on Iraq. To what extent do you think spirituality is welcome and part of the peace movement?

MF: Well, it is interesting, because traditionally in America, there hasn't really been a strong Left. If I go to Europe, for example, if I am in Italy, they have very strong parties today that are still recognized as being Communist or Socialist or Green or some other left-wing party. They are very legitimized and recognized. In America, those parties have always been left out of the process and have been pushed to the side and have been really ostracized.

MICHAEL
FRANTI

21 ▶

During the fifties with the whole McCarthy era, the Left really took on a bad connotation in this country. Even today the word "liberal" is this evil word. Even Left-leaning people don't like to consider themselves as such.

In part because of that, the Left has at times been very dogmatic. Some people are very strict about Marx's idea that religion is the opiate of the masses. And then on the other hand you have the religious Right, which is trying to force religious ideology down people's throats, often in a very mean-spirited way. The bombing of abortion clinics, the anti-gay and lesbian sentiment, and the very pro-war stances and very anti-Muslim stances are part of the religious Right. So, we have two extremes.

But people are really questioning their lives. We live in this nation where we have virtually anything we want. Computers, music, movies, homes, cars, food. In overabundance. And yet, people are still stressed out, unhappy with their jobs, unhappy with their lives, unhappy with their relationships, and a lot of times when we move into social justice work, we carry all of that unhappiness into our work. In order for us to manifest peace, we have to begin to manifest that peace in ourselves, in our hearts.

Somewhere along the line, the idea of spirituality takes place in the hearts and minds of everybody who is in the movement. Because we go out in the street and we raise our voices and think the world is going to change and we come home the next day and read the newspaper and it says that there were five thousand when there were five *hundred* thousand of us in the street! We see the president is doing the same stuff he was doing yesterday. He is not calling us saying, "You guys were right. I saw your protest and I'm changing my mind." It doesn't work like that. So, we have to endure. And in order to endure, we have to be able to breathe and say, "Okay, how are we going to face today and move on?" That is what spirituality is.

I feel like the more that there are spiritual leaders who provide ideas for people and options for people to explore, then the better off the movement will be. I don't feel like the movement has to all decide one day that we're all going to follow one leader or one religion. But each of us in our heart has to decide how we are going to hold on to love. How is it that we're going to let go of our attachments? How is it that we are going to learn to practice loving-kindness in every step of our life? Because at the end of the day, we might not ever see the goals that we are trying to attain. We might not see a world without militarism. We might not ever see a world where there is fair trade.

We might not see a world where there is environmental love and justice taking place. So maybe all we have is the relationships between the people that we make posters with. And if that's the case, if that's all we're going to get out of this, then we better make those relationships loving relationships. If that is all we get, then the means by which we do things becomes even more important than the end. So, we have to learn and practice those loving practices along the way.

JM: I think that in spiritual traditions this notion of long-term view is very important, as well as interconnectedness.

MF: A lot of us in this country are used to instant gratification. We see it on television and buy it in the store and it's immediately here to make us happy. Things don't really work that way in the larger world.

I like to tell this story. A butterfly is sitting in this tree and a bird comes up and says, "Mr. Butterfly, you've been here your whole life. All five days. And I've got a question — Is this tree alive?" And the butterfly says, "I have been here my whole life, all five days, and I've never once seen the tree move. So, this tree has got to be dead." Five years later, the tree has borne fruit and animals and humans have eaten and shared the fruit and used it to fertilize the tree. The little seedlings have grown up and the roots are connected to create a family and the branches have grown wide and the tree has given off so much oxygen that we, in turn, have breathed in, and given our $CO_2$ back to the tree so that the tree could breathe out. We've had this whole relationship with the tree. The tree has grown so much. And the same thing goes with social movements. If we just look at things in one lifetime, or in the time of one generation, we would think that things were not alive.

But, look historically and see where things were in the 1950s. We can move forward, recognizing that things don't change on their own. They only change in the direction that we choose to help them to move. We are part of this massive glacier. This glacier is kind of sloping down the mountain into this abyss of militarism and environmental toxicity and anger. Now, we on the other side have to begin to shift this glacier. All of us on this planet are beginning to see that the human interests and the natural interests and the spiritual interests need to begin to take a priority over the corporate and the military and the materialistic interests.

JM: There is a lot of talk among people I know about this being a very dark time. There is a lot of fear and anger and, along with that, there is potential for learning a lot and connecting with people. How would you describe this time?

MF: There is always the power of the destroyer in the universe. The destroyer has to do its thing for there to be new growth and new life. There has to be that balance. You could look at our current situation and see us as moving toward a U.S. empire that makes subjects of every person and every animal and every tree on this planet. Or you could look at our current situation as giving the world this wonderful gift of a wake-up call to say, "Hey, what direction do you really want to go?" Do we really want this to be a militaristic planet or not? Now it is time for us to speak up.

When I was in Germany, I asked people, "How did this Holocaust take place here?" And they said, "It wasn't that there were so many bad people in Germany. It was that all of the good people were afraid to speak out." That is what we have in this country today. Now is the time for good people to raise their voices, whether at the water cooler at work or at the dinner table at home, whether at a store or looking at the newspaper rack or out in the street in protest or writing letters. Whatever we can do to raise our voice, now is the time.

JM: On your latest CD you sing, "Even our worst enemies deserve music." You also sing about not being afraid. There is a whole song, "Don't be afraid of the preacher, don't be afraid of your teacher or your father. Don't be afraid of your best friend, don't be afraid of your worst friend." We have this tendency to divide the world into people who are making us happy and people who are making us unhappy and we want to get rid of the people that are making us unhappy. A lot of young people I talk to seem to have some new fear and anxiety about the future. They believe things are not looking like they are getting better. What is your main message to young people in the United States?

MF: My main message has always been to be yourself. A lot of times you hear the word "diversity" and we think that diversity is at a school or at a job. You have some black people there and you have some brown people there and some different ethnic groups. But really, diversity is within each of us. Some of us like to paint. Some of us like to draw. Some of us like to walk.

Some of us like to paint and draw and walk at the same time. Some of us like to do different things. So, we each have diversity in us that goes well beyond our ethnic groupings or our economic groupings or our political groupings. A lot of times we are afraid to show that. Especially as teenagers. The main worry that we have is that we want to fit in with other people.

So, throughout life, we are on a journey to undo all the layers that we piled on during our youth to cover us from being the people that we really are. My music is a manifestation of the diversity within. That is why my music is part rock, part funk, part soul, sometimes it's sad and sometimes it's happy. It's just me attempting to be myself in an artistic way. And that is my message to other young people. It is okay just to be yourself.

MICHAEL
FRANTI

25 ▶

## Michael Franti Selected Discography

*Home* – 1994 (Capitol Records)
*Chocolate Supa Highway* – 1997 (Capital Records)
*Michael Franti Live at the Baobab* – 1999 (Boo Boo Wax Records)
*Stay Human* – 2001 (Boo Boo Wax Records)
*Songs from the Front Porch* – 2003 (Boo Boo Wax Records)
*Everyone Deserves Music* – 2003 (Boo Boo Wax Records)

# STRANGE ANGEL

## An Interview with Laurie Anderson

Hello goodbye
To all the men and women
Who pass through her port
Into the open ocean
Just another speckle on horizon
Just another speckle in the sea
Cool water
Cool wind
Freedom is a scary thing
Not many people really want it
—from "Statue of Liberty" by Laurie Anderson

LAURIE ANDERSON is a performance artist, filmmaker, violinist, composer, visual artist, and author. She is a contemporary storyteller, with a knack for offering views of reality that come from unexpected sources and voices, but are still recognizably our lives. In over thirty years as a musician, she has continued to create music and performance that surprise and provoke. She has designed musical instruments, created art installations, recorded over a dozen albums, and toured internationally as a multimedia performance artist.

Laurie Anderson was born in 1947 in Chicago and raised with seven siblings. She studied art with Sol LeWitt, graduated from Columbia University with an MFA in Art in 1972, and soon after, presented her first performance art piece, an outdoor concert for car horns titled "Automotive." She later designed the "tape bow violin" – a violin with a recording head built into it, so that a bow of audiotape can be drawn across it and amplified.

In 1980, Laurie Anderson recorded the song "O Superman" and it rose to number two on the British pop charts. It later appeared on her first album *Big Science*. A single vocal syllable, rhythmically pulsing, begins the song and carries through the whole piece. Over the minimalist music, her voice can be heard:

> This is the hand
> the hand that takes
> Here come the planes
> They're American planes
> Made in America.

In 1981, she performed in an Anti-Inaugural Ball for Ronald Reagan. She performed with Paul Simon and Bruce Springsteen at a 1987 benefit concert for New York Children's Health Project and at many concerts to raise money to help those with AIDS. She has also been a strong voice against censorship and in favor of increasing arts funding, making numerous public appearances, including a televised debate on CNN in 1992. Anderson is a founding member of the Women's Action Coalition. Instead of doing a music video for her 1989 album *Strange Angels*, she created a series of short "personal service announcements" on various topics, including military spending, the national debt, the national anthem, women's salaries, technology, and television.

Her latest work, *The End of the Moon*, is partly a report from her time at NASA, where in 2003 she was the first (and last) artist-in-residence. The piece is also a look at the relationships between war, aesthetics, spirituality and consumerism, and an exploration of the question, "Who taught you what beauty is?" "My plan," she wrote in the program notes for the show, "is to invent a language that will explore the contemporary meanings of freedom and time." *The End of the Moon* is the second in a planned trilogy of solo performance works, following *Happiness* (2002), which was based partly on her time working at a McDonald's in New York City and living on an Amish farm.

I first experienced *The End of the Moon* in May 2004, when Anderson performed the piece as a work-in-progress in Santa Cruz, California. A week after the U.S. presidential elections, I saw a finished version of the piece in Berkeley.

*The End of the Moon* explores, among other things, the events of September 11, 2001. In the piece she says: "At the beginning of the war with Iraq we were asking, 'Why does everybody hate us? Is it because we are rich, free and democratic?' No. It's like in high school when the beautiful girl says, 'People hate me because I'm beautiful.' No, actually people hate you because you're a jerk!".

▼ ▼ ▼ ▼

**John Malkin**: You have said that the title of your latest work, *The End of the Moon*, stems from a sense of loss, and that what you feel you have lost is a country. Tell me about that.

**Laurie Anderson**: *The End of the Moon*, is a report of my artist-in-residency at NASA. It begins there, but then twists around here and there, going this way and that. Generally, our exploration of space—or outer space—is directed to the future, to frontiers and pioneers. It is really kind of strange that we focus on where we are going to go and what we are going to find instead of thinking of our ability to explore the objects in space, the most impossible, ancient things ever. For me, the piece connects to people's sense of direction and aspiration.

When I was a kid, I remember really clearly that it was a very exciting kind of destiny to get to space, and a huge challenge. Of course, under the surface of the glamour of John F. Kennedy saying, "We are going to go to space and discover this and that," there was a huge amount of competition and desire for ownership and safety. There were military reasons for our space exploration and it was very aggressively pursued.

But the government and scientists and the media framed it in such a positive way that everyone went, "Yeah! Great idea!" Instead of noticing that this was another "How The West Was Won" exercise in which the military goes out into the frontier so that we can own everything we see. It's Cortez all over again. See something you like? Grab it!

There is less focus on discovery in space these days because there isn't that much glamour associated with it anymore. Once in a while we make it to Mars. NASA tries to show people what it is we are looking for, but it seems like the European space agencies are doing projects that strike people as more romantic: Saturn's moon and looking around at Titan. NASA's projects tend to be more about rolling vehicles around. That's great, too, because the dream is to find other life.

So, *The End of the Moon* had to do with finding our aspirations, as much as anything. I was writing about NASA and fragmented language and I didn't realize it at the time, but I felt an enormous sadness. The sadness came through in this piece even though I didn't really think that was what I was doing.

You know, one of the times that you really learn what you're doing is when you try to translate it into another language. I am working on this project in Japan now, for the 2005 World Exposition in Japan. I've used about ten little pieces from *The End of the Moon* as texts for a film I am making. One of the pieces has this little sentence about loss:

> I knew I'd lost something
> I just couldn't put my finger on it.

And I paired that with this image of Mount Fuji.

The Japanese translator asked me, "Now tell me, when you are talking about what you lost, what did you lose?" At first I just said, "Well, you know, it's just about losing things in general. Things that you value." But then I thought more about it and said, "Actually, I wrote that at the beginning of the war with Iraq and it was about the United States." And he said, "Well, when a Japanese person hears those words and sees this image of Fuji, we think of what it means to have a place and to lose it. We think of what the symbol means." So my unconscious was working overtime. I didn't even know what I was talking about until I fumbled along. I might as well have put these words next to a big old frayed American flag!

In translation, much of the common ground that I thought I had in working on that project had to be examined. One of the other stories in the film was about revenge and an angry God. It was about this sort of justice. The translator said, "You know, I have to tell you, when you say *justice*, we say *harmony*. And when you say *rights*, we say *responsibility*." I thought, "Whoa, this is going to be a really hard conversation because it involves such different premises than our heritage of Greek heroes and egos and all of the 'me, me, me' stuff."

When we would have a disagreement with the Japanese team, somebody wouldn't say, "Dave is angry." Instead, they might say, "There is anger in this room." Working with the Japanese, the porous quality of human nature became more and more vivid to me. And that is something I am really trying to represent in this work that I am doing in Japan. Not that I really know how to do it, but I am doing what I can because I'm much more interested in translation and connection than I am in self-expression.

JM: One of the most chilling and memorable parts of *The End of the Moon* is when you discuss the current war in Iraq and say, "This war will never be over. It will just keep moving from place to place." What do you think is the root cause of our ongoing wars on this planet?

LA: What a huge question! I did a little tour with a band in the fall of 2001. In people's minds, a lot of the songs were strangely about that. One of the songs was talking about American planes smashing into things. People said, "Well, this is all about September 11. How did you, how did you know all of that stuff was going to happen?" I said, "Well, you know, the fiction is that the war ever ended." We are presented with this series of chapters in a war. The Gulf War was conceived as a dramatic thing that had a beginning, middle, and an end. "Oh, over! Okay!" But that conflict is the same conflict we're in today.

I wrote the song about the planes smashing into things, "O Superman," in 1980, during the Iran-Contra affair. That affair was part of this same collision of the West and Islamic East. And here in America, we keep thinking that these are just a bunch of wars, instead of stepping back and seeing that this is an ongoing, enormous thing. Two very different ways of viewing the world are colliding.

I was working with the Japanese translator on the song about the angry god. This little song is about revenge and concealment. In the story, the god is hiding and issuing commands to people from a burning bush. This god keeps telling the men and women to hide. "Hide like I do," he says, "in an abandoned car. Hide in the eyes of a newborn child."

The Japanese translator asked, "What's a burning bush?" So I asked him where the angry gods lived in his culture and he said they lived in caves in the mountains." I said, "Okay. Make it a cave in a mountain." Everyone has these angry gods, they just don't take them as seriously in Japan. The thing is that Western gods are really into revenge and a certain kind of concealment.

I don't know everything this war is about and how to avoid it. I would be the last person in the world to know how to avoid something like that. But I do know one thing we could do to make everything a little less horrible. One thing we could do is to permit people to come into this country. We could open our doors a little bit more rather then keeping them slammed shut.

Like many musicians, I am on a circuit that is in a different world. It is a cultural circuit of cities. When I perform in San Francisco, it reminds me of Berlin. It is an urban trail that has to do with music and dance and theatre and culture. That has not yet been destroyed. But for so many people now, including musicians, it is harder and harder to come to the United States. This is going to have disastrous results over a few years. There will be less and less interaction between Americans and people from the rest of the world. It is very dangerous to be this cut off.

I am really afraid that there will be less cultural cross-communication and pollination. Music allows us to understand other people in such a deep way. Dance, too. I see a Sufi spinning and think, "I know ecstasy." We are all trying to get that. Whether you have to buy drugs or breakdance on your head, which is just kind of a Sufi upside-down, really, we're all trying to get to that place of joy. How do we get there? One of the ways is through exquisite things like dance and music. Cutting off cultural contact with the rest of the world is a very bad idea.

JM: How does spirituality fit into this? Science and politics try to change things by transforming material outside of ourselves, while spiritual traditions emphasize transforming our internal experience. What do you see as the relationship between social change and spiritual growth?

LA: Boy, these are not small questions! I have to speak from my own experience and one of things that I have been startled by is the spread of Buddhism in the United States. It is incredible how many roots have been set down over the last thirty years. You can go from Wisconsin to Florida and there are these Zen centers and meditation places. And this is arguably the most materialistic country in the world. I don't know yet what difference that will make.

Before the November 2004 Presidential election, I traveled in a lot of states that supported George W. Bush and found that one of the things that attracted a lot of the students that I met to him was what they felt to be his sincerity and warmth, and his commitment to moral values. They thought his opponent seemed chilly. It is unbelievable how perceptions can be changed and manipulated through media. I personally saw the November 2004 election as an American-style coup, in which the media and the money were controlled by people in power.

I'm not particularly a conspiracist, but I do think that the American political style is to control people and convince them of something that is obviously the opposite of what is going on. A lot of televisions were turned on and minds were changed without any relationship to the truth.

Two years ago, I did an audio diary series for French radio. I recorded a few minutes of audio everyday for about six months. It was an editing nightmare! I decided to complete this project by walking from Milan to Paris, just to see what would happen. But there was this problem of the Alps. So, I decided to get to Paris another way. I had about ten days. I was polling some people to see how I could get there. A friend of mine, Chris Marker, a French filmmaker who made a beautiful film, *La Jetée*, suggested a route from Charleville to Paris. Charleville is his birthplace, but it is also the birthplace of Arthur Rimbaud, who wrote beautiful things about freedom and walking. People told me that Charleville was a really dull town and that Rimbaud had always been running away. So, I thought I'd take that runaway route to Paris and see what would happen.

And while walking, I kept thinking about something George W. Bush had said, not to harp on the poor guy. I had heard a speech where he said something like "The founding fathers of the U.S. were men of God and country." And I thought, "They weren't! In fact, they were the opposite!" These guys were men of the Enlightenment. They were reading [François-Marie Arouet de] Voltaire and [Denis] Diderot. They wanted to separate church and state. That was their big idea, and yet Bush was saying the exact opposite.

Anyway, I thought that it would be especially nice to walk through France because in the late eighteenth century, France resurrected an incredible idea of freedom. At the founding of America, the founders looked over to France and took a lot of ideas and adapted them for the Constitution. So I thought of my journey as an homage to the French and this idea of freedom and individuality. I thought I'd walk through the French countryside, on my way to Paris. One slight problem: we're hated in the French countryside and in Paris! [Laughter] So, I got an ambassador! The French love dogs and I have a little dog named Lolabelle, which is kind of a French name. I took her along to break the ice. "Just passing through. Hello!" I just wanted to be walking through that countryside.

I am inspired by ideals. And I find the ideal of the French revolution incredibly inspiring. Even though I find the emphasis on individual rights to be a little troubling. What about responsibilities? Sometimes all that emphasis on individual rights tramples other people.

In the United States, freedom and religious belief have become so intricately entwined that we are even capable of having a president who doesn't understand the difference. Spirituality and religion are quite different, but I guess that when I think of spirituality, I just don't think of groups. I only think of single people making an effort. Or is that true? I don't know. Let's go on to your next question. I'm a rambler, as you might have guessed.

JM: I would like to hear more about how Buddhism has affected you in your life and in your work. As Buddhism travels around the world, it both affects the place it travels to and is changed by that place. I wonder if you have any thoughts about what the United States of America might be offering Buddhism?

LA: It depends on the kind of Buddhism that you're talking about. But I think that if I had to make a really silly generalization, I would say that the American style of informality is certainly affecting the Zen traditions here. Just personally, I'm sure that it is just some kind of leftover attempt to be a bad girl, when I am in any kind of a Zen temple, I find it very frustrating that everything is so neat and perfectly asymmetrical. It makes me crazy! You don't find a lot of guffawing or giggling in a Zen temple. There is much more restraint.

It is wonderful that there are so many varied traditions. Personally, I am drawn to sloppiness and fun and so, in many ways, more attracted to Tibetan Buddhism. Just because they've got such a great sense of humor! I love to laugh and they do, too. Tibetan Buddhism has a kind of crazy joy and anarchy in it that I find very, very appealing. Being an American, I feel guilty about that, of course. Sometimes, I think maybe I need discipline and should force myself to have it. But I'm not sure that forcing myself is a good idea because I have just spent my whole life forcing myself to do things. I've spent a lot of my life making lures and traps and trying to find ways to accomplish things. Maybe I should just try to find out what I am naturally attracted to.

I remember the Dalai Lama at Madison Square Gardens in New York. It was great to see the marquee because you'd see, "Wrestling," and some kind of "Dog Show," and then, "The Dalai Lama." I thought, "This is heaven. I'm living in heaven now! New York is finally getting it!" You know? They've really got their priorities together.

There were a lot of monks from Tibet who were in New York at that time and they were clumping around in those brown shoes and their robes. They were living in midtown in Catholic monasteries. I remember a photograph from a *New York Times* article at the time. It was a picture of the monks sitting at a long table having a breakfast of cornflakes. The Catholic monks were on one side and the Tibetans on the other. There was a big crucifix at the end of the table. It was five in the morning and they were just happy to be there.

The *Times* reporter asked the Tibetans, "I see the crucifix there. What do you think of Jesus Christ?" There was this emaciated, horrifying crucifix hanging over their cornflakes. The Tibetans said, "Oh, we like him!" I thought, "These are people that are so unbelievably endearing and open and happy." That is the thing that I think Americans share with Tibetans, even if it's just on a silly level. Happiness is very, very important to Americans. I don't know how we achieve it. We have lots of wretched interpretations of what that means. But we *are* the only country that has the word in our constitution. It means something. It's not just "everyone will be equal" or "justice will be served." It is "the pursuit of happiness." And these guys, these forefathers, even though they weren't saying, "The king is God," they did have some sense that people could look for what they wanted to look for.

JM: It sounds like you view a link between freedom and happiness. On the song "Statue of Liberty," from the *Life On A String* album, there is the line, "Freedom is a scary thing, not many people want it." I wonder what your thoughts are about what it is that is scary about freedom and, maybe also, about happiness?

LA: Well, I wrote that for students because I happened to be, at that point, talking to a lot of students. They were always saying things like, "I really want to be an artist, but what would my parents say, and my friends?" I said, You know, I hate to tell you this, but not that many people actually care what you do. Of course, a couple of people do. But, they care what you do about as much as you care about what they do. It's not going to rock their world if you become an artist. It is hard to make a decision like that. It is easier to say that social pressures prevent you. It is terrifying then, because who then is responsible? Not mom and dad and your friends. You! And who could step up to that plate? That's a really big one. A lot of people are scared of the responsibility that comes with freedom. The idea that you're the only one in charge is too much for people. I don't know what that means in a larger picture of what Buddhism will be like in the United States eventually.

It is easier to use the usual goals of success and the so-called happiness that is supposed to come with it just through accumulation of stuff. There is a huge amount of pressure that says that you just have to get material wealth and then you'll be really, really happy. And I think we're dumb enough to fall for it. I have fallen for it a trillion times! I walk like a donkey following a carrot on a stick. But at some point I just couldn't lure myself further with these promises of what I was going to get. Because every time I would get what I had worked so hard for, I would say, "That's it? That is what I have been working for? That wasn't worth what I had to do to get it!"

I suppose that from my own dissapointment, I learned what really matters to me. Now, I am somebody who is really privileged. I am able to make music and do a lot of different kinds of projects and I'm really grateful for that. But I am also very aware that I am a lot more porous than I thought. I am a lot less interested in trying to prop up some kind of big ego.

JM: After you performed recently in Santa Cruz, you met with a group of students and spoke a little about silence and the role of silence in your life and in your work. You actually stopped for maybe one or two minutes and allowed silence to be in the room. Tell me more about silence.

LA: One of the exercises that I like to do, just to remind myself how much I need to learn, is I try to use the wrong sense. For example, you can hear with your hands, with touch. Deaf people do it all of the time. But you can't, for example, smell with your eyes. No matter how hard you try. And so, it reminds me of all the things that we don't know. We have no idea how they work. Ninety percent of the universe is totally invisible. We don't know what it's made of! Wandering around in the ten percent that we sort of get, and to the rest of it, we're oblivious. And, why would we know that it's ninety percent? Why isn't it ninety-nine point nine percent? It easily could be.

I try to listen as well as I can. In fact, trying to sometimes use one sense exclusively. So, one day I might use just my ears. It's as if I'm in a silent movie. On the days that I use my eyes, it is almost like sound drops away to nothing. Everything I learn has to be visual. And you can sharpen things so much that way. You can really sharpen your senses. And then, when you decide, "I'm going to use all five," it is almost overwhelming. You realize that you have access to this incredible amount of information, if you want it. Most of the time, we don't do that. We are busy. Or we have to go over there and we don't see the advantage in being aware. So, a lot of skills that allowed us to survive as creatures are, in certain ways, atrophying, as we sit at computers and don't move, don't listen, don't really look, except in rectangles. Our depth perception starts becoming less acute.

So, I think it is really important, because technology certainly isn't going to go away, to use technology to sharpen our senses, instead of depending on machines that dull them. If we rely too much on technology, we become unable to receive new information, because we've closed ourselves into a box. Anyone who has been depressed knows that. That is feeling like nothing can come in and everything looks gray and it doesn't sound interesting. I'm not really talking about meditation. Meditation is sharpening of the mind in another way. I am talking about the danger in closing down and just not letting anything in.

JM: In a 1992 interview you did with John Cage (for *Tricycle Magazine*), you talk about your own confusion, at that time, with incorporating politics into your art. Cage thought that you could do that. In fact, he thought that you *were* doing that. He also said that, "Rather than complaining about politics, I think that we should become actively disinterested in politics." Tell me about how you currently address social change issues in your life and in your work and how that has evolved in your music and art.

LA: Maybe this is a dream come true for Cage. A lot of people are not so interested—they are quite disinterested—in politics. They have really shut themselves off at the moment. I don't think that everybody does that. There are a few people who are just so angry that they're beginning to do things that they wouldn't have done before and becoming more politically active. Most people I know are becoming less involved in the world. They feel defeated and tired.

JM: Your current music and performance seems like a return to simplicity, in terms of less technology, less voices, and even the material itself. Is this a reflection of your feelings about contemporary society and this "speed revolution" we are experiencing these days, where technology means every-thing happens so fast? Also, you mentioned your intention of being goal-less. How are these ideas being reflected in your current work?

LA: I just cannot do a multimedia show these days. It seems preposterous to me. I don't know why. Just a bunch of screens and stuff, you push but-tons and everything's a go. I don't know. I just see them everywhere and I am never moved by them. In fact, the bigger the machine, the less I am moved by it. It's true, by the time you mobilize the many different kinds of elements—visual and music—it moves slower. And becomes blander. It doesn't seem to become more beautiful and spectacular for me. I can think of exceptions to that. I have seen a lot of big performances with projection lately and they just leave me cold. Maybe it is just that I am looking at them super-critically.

I think that you can do more flexible things and you can be more subtle if you're quicker. And quicker for me means the little things you can do as a per-former to improvise. For me, this is the ultimate fun because, in *The End of the Moon*, you can choose between a bunch of foot pedals or programs. It's not linear. I ran into someone in Boston who used to do the front-of-house engi-neering for shows for me and she said, "Wow, there is no beginning or end now. You just go here or go there, you're selecting stuff." That really, for me, makes it so much fun, to make a decision on the spot. Wing it.

Although, in Boston, I really did have to wing it and I wasn't so sure I loved it! A few minutes into the show, the sound system crashed and the lights went out and an announcement came on saying, "Leave the theater now!"

Half of the people thought it was part of the show. I knew it obviously wasn't. My first thought was, "A bomb." I thought, "Let me just check if this is real." It was eerie in a big theater to not have a microphone and try to get across to people that they should just chill. But, the stage manager said, "No. We have to get everybody out right now!" There was a snowstorm! They went out and when they came back I picked up where I was and five minutes later, the lights came on again and there were all of these police and a huge fight was going on. It was a strange evening!

As soon as it was over, I realized, "That wasn't so bad." Of course, it wasn't like the equipment crashed and we had to say, "Well, nothing works. Goodnight. Sorry." Would I do that? I am really proud that I do this myself. I've got a big ego investment in this. "Yes, I am the roadie and the performer!"

**JM**: How much of the music that you're playing in *The End of the Moon* is improvised?

**LA**: All of it.

**JM**: Really?

**LA**: Oh, all of it. And that's what makes it a thrill. And sometimes I will hit another foot pedal to go into a whole other sound and it makes it so much fun for me. Or I will skip something or totally revise it, play it in another key. Or not play anything like the last time. It really makes this possible for me. Otherwise, you're kind of stuck. The music varies a lot more than the text. The text does, too. I change it around, but not as much as that. It makes it really fun to experiment with.

**JM**: One of my favorite lines from your music is, "Paradise is exactly like where you are right now, only much, much better." It is a funny statement. It makes me laugh. But it is also a serious statement. I think that a lot of us walk around believing, without realizing it with such clarity, "This is great, but if only it were a bit better…" Or, "This is great and I want more!" Or, "If this would only happen less." Are we in paradise?

**LA**: Yup. We are in it. This is it. This is it. And I can't think of how to improve it. It is all here. And that is a big comfort to me, in a lot of ways. It is not always as obvious at some times as at other times. Unquestionably, we are in paradise. I guess it has to do, really, with accounting. When I stop measuring and saying, "This is a lot better" or "not as good" or "I need more or less," I realize that it is a strange kind of accounting that I would really like to drop. I was doing that right after 9/11 with people. And I hadn't realized that I was doing that with *people*. I know that at parties, people kind of go, "Oh, that person is not going to get me anywhere, so I'm not going to say anything to them." I know that there's lots of levels, where accounting comes into play, but I didn't realize I was doing it.

I discovered that I was doing this when I was walking along. It was night and I saw someone on the other side of the street and a week before, I would have crossed the street and kind of glanced over my shoulder or made sure I was not going to run into this person. I didn't feel like doing that at all. And I didn't. And why? Because on some other level, I thought, "That person might be a bad guy, but he wouldn't have done *that* – flown a plane into a building. He wouldn't have done that." It is a whole other scale that I had inside and I wasn't realizing that I was applying that scale to people. There was something going on. The lymbic mind, the snake mind, that was going, "That one's dangerous," or "that one's not going to hurt you." When you are trying to decide whether it is good, I don't know.

Working with, and getting to know, NASA researchers taught me a lot about how to evaluate what *good* is, or whether it is enough or not. Because they reminded me that I don't know exactly what I'm looking for. The classic example, in the world of science, is Einstein rejecting some of his theories. Why? Because they weren't beautiful. Wait a second! Then, what are you looking for? Is it beautiful if it is symmetrical or right or big? What is beautiful for you? And what makes you stop and say, "That's it." So, that is why beauty is a big part of *The End of the Moon*. It did make me realize that maybe I really only understand *style*. There are plenty of things that we all agree are beautiful today. And those other things that are boring today, they were beautiful yesterday. And they were interesting. They were art! Now they're not even art, they're just junk. Or they are cheap art, discount art.

**JM**: In *The End of the Moon*, you talk about being the artist-in-residence at NASA and these images of outer space they put out all over the world. You tell us that people at NASA actually picked the colors depicted in the images. What did they say when you asked them how they'd decided on what colors to use?

LA: They said, "We thought people would like them." I have come to think of that as not being as radical as I imagined at the time. Anyone who takes a digital photograph knows that—their Christmas picture that looks a little dull, people are sitting around, the light's making them look a little green— hey, no problem! You can make it look like the fire is burning in the fireplace and everyone has rosy cheeks. You can take all of those bluish, green icky things out. So, why wouldn't they do that with the image of a star being born? Fix it up. We all do that, constantly. Or even if it is not a photograph, we imagine that things were simpler than they actually were. Or more beautiful and wonderful. It is probably some kind of great happiness filter that we apply so that it's not so dreadful to keep on living.

JM: You mentioned earlier that Tibetan Buddhism has a sense of anarchy. I wonder if anarchist philosophy resonates with you, in terms of how societies are structured and how people organize themselves and their worlds?

LA: It completely does! It always has, from my childhood. It probably has to do with coming from a family of eight kids and things always being kind of a mess. One of our favorite things to do was a game we played only on Sundays called "Rat's Nest." You would take the *Chicago Tribune* and rip it into as many pieces as it could possibly be ripped into and make these rats' nests out of them and burrow around in them. That was so unbelievably satisfying. To take all of that information and then shred it and just live in it. And make a mess of it! It was put into a certain order, it was kind of arbitrary. Style section versus the political section. Why not reverse it? It seemed so inevitable.

So, I always gravitated toward anything that would mess things up a little bit. I loved using objects for things that they weren't meant for. That was very satisfying for me. I just don't like to have everything figured out for me. I like to change it. I am sure that is a preference. I know that a lot of my friends hated stuff like that. They would love to be in a place where everything was organized for them; "Bedtime is eight." You know, they knew what they were going to have for breakfast. That, for me, was a kind of torture. It is just two different ways of living, as there are trillions of different ways of living. I'm not trying to say one is better than another. There are just so many different ways to be in the world.

# Laurie Anderson Selected Discography

*O Superman* – 1981 (Warner Brothers Records)

*Big Science* – 1982 (Warner Brothers Records)

*Mister Heartbreak* – 1984 (Warner Brothers Records)

*United States Live* – 1984 (Warner Brothers Records)

*Home of the Brave* – 1986 (Warner Brothers Records)

*Strange Angels* – 1989 (Warner Brothers Records)

*Bright Red* – 1994 (Warner Brothers Records)

*The Ugly One with the Jewels and Other Stories* – 1995 (Warner Brothers Records)

*Life on A String* – 2001 (Nonesuch Records)

*Talk Normal: Laurie Anderson Anthology* – 2001 (Warner Bros./Rhino Entertainment)

*Live In New York* – 2002 (Nonesuch Records)

*The Record of the Time* – 2002 (Musée d'Art Contemporain, Lyon)

# ROCK IS COOL,
# BUT THE STRUGGLE IS BETTER

## An Interview with the Indigo Girls

I kicked up the dirt, and I said to my neighbor,

"We keep making it worse, we keep getting it wrong."

He tucked in his shirt, he stood a little bit straighter,

He said, "We need a few less words, dear, we need a few more guns."

But will it bring us together,

Can we call from the mountain to the valley below?

Can we make it better,

Do we tether the hawk or do we tether the dove?

—from "Tether" by the Indigo Girls

EMILY SALIERS AND AMY RAY, the two singer/songwriters of the Indigo Girls, have devoted their careers to making great folk-rock music. Their deepest intention is to speak out for social, economic, and environmental justice and to contribute to the well-being of the planet and all of its inhabitants. Perhaps one key to their success has been the diverse sound that Ray and Saliers bring to the Indigo Girls. They write their songs separately and then perform and record together. Saliers's insightful lyrics and sweet melodies are informed by a Christian spirituality. She and her father, Don, have recently written *A Song to Sing, A Life to Live: Reflections on Music as Spiritual Practice*, about the healing power of music and the sacred and truth-revealing qualities present in music of many styles and cultures.

Ray has brought to the Indigo Girls a punk rock edge, with her gravelly voice and Do-It-Yourself sensibilities. In 1990, Ray established Daemon Records, a nonprofit label with an emphasis on promoting a range of independently-minded, socially-critical, and musically diverse artists such as

Kristen Hall, Ellen James Society, Utah Phillips, James Hall, John Trudell, and Holland's punk band, Bambix. Amy's first solo album, *Stag*, was released by Daemon Records in 2001. Guest artists on the album, including Joan Jett, Kate Schellenbach (Luscious Jackson), and Josephine Wiggs (Breeders), add to the raw under-produced sound and hard rock flavor.

Emily Saliers was born in 1963 in New Haven, Connecticut and Amy Ray was born in Atlanta, Georgia in 1964. The two met when Saliers' family moved to Decatur, Georgia when Ray was in the fifth grade. They began making music together in high school, calling themselves Saliers and Ray or the B-Band. They played at open-mic nights at local bars and in 1981 they recorded their first tape, *Tuesday's Children*, in Ray's basement.

The two went off to different colleges, but returned to Atlanta in 1984. In 1985 they were performing together again and settled on the name Indigo Girls. The first official release using that name was the seven-inch single *Crazy Game*, followed by a 1987 six-track EP. In 1987, the Indigo Girls released their album, *Strange Fire*, and in 1988, they signed a record deal with Epic Records.

In 1989 they released the self-titled *Indigo Girls*. The album, which featured REM vocalist Michael Stipe, went platinum, selling over one million records by 1991. The Indigo Girls have been nominated for numerous Grammy Awards and won the 1989 Grammy Award for Best Contemporary Folk Recording. They were also featured in the Whoopi Goldberg film *Boys on the Side* and took part in the revival of Andrew Lloyd Weber's *Jesus Christ Superstar*.

The Indigo Girls have given their time, energy, and music to a variety of social and political struggles including opposing the U.S. war in Iraq, stopping the development of nuclear weapons, and the burying of nuclear waste on sacred Native American sites, like Yucca Mountain in Nevada. They have long supported gay and lesbian rights, gun control, farmworkers' rights, and a moratorium on the death penalty. They have also done a series of benefit concerts as part of the Honor the Earth Tour, in 1995, 1997, 2000, and 2004. Honor the Earth creates awareness and support for environmental justice and the preservation of indigenous knowledge.

When I caught up with the Indigo Girls' road manager backstage at the Civic Auditorium in Santa Cruz, he laid out the band's schedule: Saliers and Ray had to eat dinner, complete guitar and vocal sound-checks, and do a couple of telephone interviews before their show. If they got a chance, they might relax for a few minutes at the hands of a masseur who was having trouble finding an available room to set up her table and candles. Though the interview was done in two parts, to accommodate their sound-checks, our discussion weaved seamlessly through rich and thoughtful territory. After our interview, Amy and Emily took the stage and played a heartfelt acoustic show for a lively audience, including a few songs from their then not-yet released album *All That We Let In.*

The Indigo Girls have combined their two voices in a harmonic call for peace and unity. We are lucky to have them.

▼ ▼ ▼ ▼ ▼

**John Malkin:** On the Indigo Girls website, there is an activism page that includes information about your involvement in Honor the Earth, a project that focuses on environmental justice and indigenous rights. At the top of the activism page it says, "Rock is cool, but the struggle is better." I am curious how you have merged your musical careers with social change work.

**Emily Saliers:** I grew up in a family where my parents were very concerned with social justice issues. My dad was at Yale at the height of the Vietnam war. I remember all of the upheaval of those times. I think my parents early on instilled in me a sense that we are part of a larger human community and that we need to alleviate suffering where we can.

Amy and I were simpatico from the very beginning. We wanted to do benefits very early on, way before we got signed to a record label. We were just members of our community seeing where we could possibly make change and also play music. The notion of activism and helping to create social change has always been integral to us as people. It was very easy to marry our activism with our music, because of the way that I was brought up.

**Amy Ray:** For me as well. I was brought up in the Methodist Church and, although that's not really my faith anymore, in the South there was this real tradition of tithing in the community, as part of a faith-based activism.

My parents are into the idea of giving back to the community, but they are very conservative. So, I took my activism in a different direction than they maybe would have chosen. Although they respect me for it. But something just appealed to me and I was very involved throughout school in student government and the idea of making change seemed a good thing, at any given moment in my life.

The idea of the first rebellion was just like a romantic thing to do and then it made sense later on. The music is something I was doing, I think, to amplify things that were inside of me. It has always been the same thing to me.

JM: Do you feel connected to any particular spiritual tradition?

AR: I have a very strong faith in the creator. I am sort of Christian because I was raised so heavily in a Christian environment in the South. It is hard to get Jesus out of your brain and your heart after that long. [Laughter] I embrace a lot of different traditions, it is kind of a mishmash inside of my head. The closest thing to spirituality for me would be more like paganism. I have a really firm belief in a creator and in positive change through activism and humanity. Prayer is important to me, it just has a different form than it did when I was young. The patriarchy of the church is hard for me to deal with and I didn't have the patience to try to stay in it and change it.

ES: I am still somewhat tied to the Christian tradition I grew up with. My father is a professor of theology and he is a minister and so we grew up in the church. But we were always encouraged to think our own thoughts, even if they wandered away from mom or dad's beliefs. I was brought up in the tradition, but I also have a very, very hard time with the institution of the church and I think that people getting together and trying to politicize or make it be an organization for their own special interests, or for the sake of power, has perverted the true message of the faith.

I like to go to church at times. There is something very powerful about being part of a community of worship. But again, in my mind, I sort of distance myself from it. Even though it means a lot to me.

I believe in a benevolent spirit, a creator, whatever you want to call it. This spirit is all around and in and through us. I believe that this is not our only life, that there is a life of the soul that came before us and carries on after us. As with nature, nothing ever dies, the energy just changes.

I definitely feel very humbled by this Great Spirit and I feel very human in the presence of this spirit. This spirit is the spirit that guides my life. There is no doubt about that.

JM: You mention humility. Your lyrics reflect this idea that there is a benefit in not knowing all of the answers. Some people involved in politics see religion as patriarchal or hierarchical. And some people who are very involved in spirituality see politics as very corrupt. Of course, there are people who are doing both. What are your feelings and thoughts about this?

AR: I don't think that the Civil Rights movement would have happened without a spiritual base. I wouldn't really have an activism without a belief in the creator. It is part and parcel of the same thing. Sometimes you need to be able to reach down into a kind of well for the courage to do all of the things that you are doing. I know some indigenous people who have done work where their life is on the line. They have to have prayer or they wouldn't have the strength that they need to take those risks.

Some religious institutions have been able to facilitate positive change, but often it seems that there are strings attached to any change that is made. Religious institutions are so powerful and have so much money. Many of those infrastructures are effective and we really would be lost without them. But at the same time they just seem to have trouble giving help unconditionally without asking for money or a spiritual commitment.

ES: I think that spiritual communities and activist communities need not be separate. There is much to be learned from both sides.

It is really hard to be a lesbian and try to participate in the church. It has been a very personal struggle of mine for a long time. I am very open and vocal about it. Luckily for me, I have mentors within a worship community who are all on my side and who want to see the church change.

The music that comes down through the centuries of worship deepens people's lives. I think it is important to have religious institutions, but the church, or the synagogue, or the mosque, or the temple has to be something that is ever evolving, that continues to question itself and that continues to ask its place in the world. That includes interpreting and reinterpreting scripture so that it is as far away from fundamentalism as you can get. Every year the Methodist Church votes on whether they are going to ordain gay people.

And it gets closer and closer to a "yes" vote. It has been very interesting to see the uproar over the Episcopalian Bishop and the church wanting to split apart, over gay issues. In time it will change and people will look back over this evolution and wonder what the problem was "all those moons ago." The right-wing part of the church, the fundamentalists, have taken over what people who aren't part of the church think about Christianity. With a few sound bites and a few condemning words, casting people's souls into hell for this and that, they have just ruined what true faith-based activism can be, to the point where I myself have felt trepidation about claiming any relationship to the church. Luckily, I know people that I can be very honest with about that and we can all grow together.

**JM**: On September 11, 2001, the two of you were on the second day of rehearsals for your CD, *Become You*. What are your thoughts and feelings about the attacks and the subsequent actions of the United States government?

**ES**: That's a lot to comment on.

**AR**: Those attacks were just huge, and the United States government has been all about some kind of idea of retaliation and vengeance. I don't believe in those values. It makes it hard to know what I feel about September 11th because now all of this other stuff has happened. We have done so many bad things.

September 11th was a terrible tragedy. It is impossible to articulate it. And I have talked with so many friends in activist communities in different parts of the world who have said, "We have lived with events like September 11th all of our lives." The attack made me feel like we were just becoming part of the world community in this very bizarre way. Our government response was just so wrong. It made me wish that we had a president who could've responded in a way that was appropriate, and taken all of those lost lives and all of that waste and all of that hate and made it into something positive, instead of playing off of it. We are in a bind now. We do all of these things now and blame it all on September 11th. The war in Iraq just has nothing to do with the attacks. Our government is behaving like a three-year-old child. Maybe it's because we are a relatively young country that we act like a little brat.

I am not good at articulating how I felt when September 11th happened. It was very scary. I just remember thinking of all the strength that it took the family and friends of people who died to remain in a place of peace and *not* want vengeance and retaliation. Their strength made me feel good about the human spirit.

ES: I remember being completely devastated by the attacks. The human suffering was just terrible. Brutality begets brutality. We played in New York not long after the attacks, and it seemed to me that there was a spirit of people really wanting peace. We sang a song about peace and when we got to the crux of the song, they clapped. They wanted healing. It wasn't like there was this sense of this bloodthirstiness.

Really, it is an awakening for our country because we'd felt we were invincible for a long time. But our responses to those attacks have been irresponsible, particularly in regards to Iraq. Many people protested that war very intensely. We stood out on the street corners of Atlanta waving peace signs. We had people shouting "Fuck you!" at us because we were protesting, people saying, "You're not Americans and you're not patriotic." All of these sound bites. This current administration has spun stories to make Americans believe that Saddam Hussein was in cahoots with Osama bin Laden and al Qaeda and these spin doctors have really made Americans believe in war.

Those people in Iraq are suffering so much. There are no weapons of mass destruction. We knew that this war was going to breed even further brutality and further misunderstanding. It is just a dark, dark time for everybody.

Every day I think about our American soldiers in Iraq and how they are suffering. They are just trying to do their job and they got sent over there. I don't think that they should've been sent over there and I resent the president for that. I don't want anybody over there to think that they are not being supported as human beings and people doing their job. They are being supported, but I just want them all to come home safe and sound and work on diplomacy.

JM: How much faith do you have in making change through the political structure that we have?

ES: There is a spectrum of activism, a spectrum of all movements, and every part and person is important. The political process is very important. It's a privilege to cast your vote and have a voice in what happens. Legislation affects people's lives. If you have anti-abortion laws passed, for example, you're going to have young women not being able to get abortions. Broadcasting legislation in 1996 allowed huge corporations to buy up all these small radio stations. So now they censor the airwaves that belong to the public and this affects all of us.

I believe in the political process, but it is not the only process. There is also the spiritual process. In the Zuni community of the Southwest, for example, they wanted to fight this company that was going to come and do mining near their sacred salt lake. This was a huge, very, very rich corporation coming in to encroach on sacred life. And the Zuni won that battle. The mining is not going to happen. It was just a small community of people who were fighting for the right thing, and they won. I believe that there is a spiritual hand in those victories.

You have to take action and be involved in the political process. And you also have to believe in grassroots activism. I have seen the importance of both with my own eyes.

JM: I notice that you and Amy seem to be particularly interested in indigenous struggles. You both went to Chiapas and had encounters with the Zapatistas, which inspired the song "Nuevas Señoritas." What draws you to the struggles for justice of indigenous peoples in the United States and elsewhere?

ES: We met Winona La Duke at an Earth Day concert back in 1990. Amy started talking to her about some of the environmental work that we've done and Winona started talking to her about the environmental work in the Native communities, and we found a way to hook up and start Honor the Earth to raise awareness and money for Native environmental groups and communities. Indian communities are sitting on all these great resources, timber, coal or even just desert where the government wants to ship nuclear waste and dump it on Indian lands. These communities are just fighting for the preservation of the Earth. Also, these small communities are very inspirational. The decision-making process takes into account the generations to come. Decisions are always community-responsible and are rarely ever made by one person.

JM: How have anarchist and punk rock values influenced your music? To what extent do you embrace these ideas and how do you see that going together with your spirituality?

ES: Patti Smith is an artist with that punk sensibility that I fully embrace and who has really influenced and inspired me. I understand the punk rock thought that you need to come out against the establishment, but I am not an anarchist. I believe that human beings need structure and some sort of system of governance, whatever it may be. I don't even know what the best system is. I understand that when people are oppressed and can trace the cause of suffering to the actions of the government, a whole movement would spring up against that kind of authority.

If you want to talk about Christianity and you want to talk about Jesus—the guy was a radical. He hung out with all types of folks. To me, the best part of his story is that he loved all kinds of different people and wanted people to be together. He didn't separate people into groups and say, "You shouldn't love this one or that one." His teachings are of benevolence and love. The punk movement comes from a little bit different spirit. Although in the end, the goal is the same—to shake it up and get everybody together. It's just the means are different.

Of course I go to stores sometimes now I and see a punk-type T-shirt that costs $100. Parts of the punk movement have been co-opted, reproduced, and commercialized and are the furthest away from the true message of punk as the far-right Christianity is from the true message of Christianity.

JM: I hear a lot in your music about lightness coming from darkness, the interconnectedness of things, and karmic responsibility. Have you been influenced in some way by Eastern philosophies or spiritual traditions?

ES: I can't say that I have been directly influenced by Eastern ways of thinking. I only have a layperson's sort of grasp of Eastern philosophy and spirituality, but I think the teachings of the Buddha about how to appreciate the simplicity of things is very beautiful.

Human experience is full of examples where lessons come out of dark periods. This can be anything from what a nation learns after a horrific war to what an individual learns about him or herself through overcoming challenges.

There are obvious lessons and gifts of light and if you continue to seek, then you will find answers. You will find answers. You have to be able to embrace all that comes at you. I don't believe in luck. I don't believe in coincidence. I think that there is a web that is woven beyond human articulation. I also believe in activism, in stacking sandbags up against all the troubles.

And I believe in the life of the soul. I don't mean we come back as another creature in another life. I just believe in long life of the soul, the transference of energy, and the continued presence of the spirits of those that have passed on. We're here on this Earth to learn and to do what we can to make the world better. Perhaps it's as simple as that.

# Indigo Girls Selected Discography

*Indigo Girls* – 1989 (Epic Records)
*Strange Fire* – 1989 (Epic Records)
*Nomads Indians Saints* – 1990 (Epic Records)
*Back on the Bus Y'All* – 1991 (Epic Records)
*Rites of Passage* – 1992 (Epic Records)
*Swamp Ophelia* – 1994 (Epic Records)
*1200 Curfews* – 1995 (Epic Records)
*Shaming of the Sun* – 1997 (Epic Records)
*Come On Now Social* – 1999 (Epic Records)
*Retrospective* – 2000 (Epic Records)
*Become You* – 2002 (Epic Records)
*All That We Let In* – 2004 (Epic Records)

# DROPPING THE BAR LINES

## An Interview with Philip Glass

Just like space
And the great elements such as earth
May I always support the life
Of all the boundless creatures
—From *Symphony No. 5* by Philip Glass.
Text from *Bodhicaryavatara* by Shantideva.

ON A NOVEMBER EVENING in 2004, I sat entranced listening to Philip Glass and the Bang On A Can ensemble perform Glass' *Music In Fifths* in San Francisco. The composition is something between an homage and an inside joke to Glass' music teachers who had warned him against ever composing music based on fifths. Of course, Glass has never been easily dissuaded from experimenting outside the box, or removing the bar lines.

Philip Glass was born on January 31, 1937 in Baltimore, Maryland. He and his two siblings were exposed to unusual music at an early age when their father, Ben Glass, would bring home albums that were not selling well at his radio repair and record shop. He wondered if his children might provide some insight into why these classical recordings of Beethoven quartets, Schubert sonatas, and Shostakovitch symphonies were not very popular with his customers.

Glass began music lessons at the age of six and took up the flute when he was eight. In his second year of high school, he was admitted to the University of Chicago, where he majored in mathematics and philosophy and worked to support himself with jobs waiting tables and loading airplanes at airports. He graduated from the university at the age of nineteen and, determined to become a composer, he moved to New York to attend the Juilliard School.

Glass studied with Vincent Persichetti, Darius Milhaud, and William Bergsma, and became interested in avante-garde composers such as Harry Partch, Charles Ives, and Henry Cowell. He then moved to Paris to study with Nadia Boulanger. In 1965, he was hired to transcribe the Indian music of Ravi Shankar into Western musical notation for a film. This encounter with Indian music transformed his view of composing, resulting in a "dropping of the bar lines."

In contrast to the Western approach to musical composition, which slices time in the same way one slices bread, Indian music is created by taking small units or beats and stringing them together. In his autobiography, *Philip Glass On Music*, Glass writes that, "This protracted encounter with one of the great traditions of world music and one of its foremost practitioners had a profound effect on me." He then traveled to North Africa, India, and the Himalayas to do further musical research. The style that Glass developed through his encounters with Eastern music is now immediately recognizable and is heard in his prolific recordings, theater pieces and film scores. In 1990, Glass and Shankar collaborated on the album *Passages*.

While in India, Glass began to study Gandhi and the "truth-force" that had motivated the social change leader. Glass' interest in social change and spirituality is apparent in his opera *Satyagraha* (1985) and the more recent *Symphony No. 5* (2000), which is based on texts from many of the world's great wisdom traditions, including the Qur'an, The New Testament, The Kumulipo, The Popul Voh, The Bhagavad Gita, and the Bodhicaryavatara. Godfrey Reggio's film trilogy of *Koyaanisqatsi*, *Powaqqatsi*, and *Naqoyqatsi* explores the relationship between humans, nature, technology, and war, and is perfectly complimented by Glass' scores.

Other film scores by Philip Glass include *The Thin Blue Line*, *A Brief History of Time*, *Mindwalk*, *The Fog of War*, and *The Hours*. His score for Martin Scorsese's *Kundun* won the L.A. Critic's Award, as well as the Academy and Golden Globe Awards for Best Original Score, and his music for Peter Weir's *The Truman Show* won a Golden Globe Award for best score in 1999. Glass has also based some of his compositions on the writings of Allen Ginsberg (*Hydrogen Jukebox*), the music of Brian Eno and David Bowie (*Low* and *Heroes* symphonies) and has collaborated with Paul Simon, David Byrne, Laurie Anderson, and Suzanne Vega on the album *Songs from Liquid Days*.

In the early 1970s, Glass co-founded the Mabou Mines Theatre Company and his own performing group, The Philip Glass Ensemble. In 1976, Glass and Robert Wilson created the opera *Einstein On The Beach*, a five hour epic and landmark in contemporary music-theater. They later worked on a number of other projects including the operas *Satyagraha*, based on the nonviolent social change movements of Gandhi and Martin Luther King, Jr., and *Akhnaten* (1987). All three of the operas focus on people who have changed the world through their ideas.

Though it was rock 'n' roll artists who received notice for their engagement in the 2004 Get-Out-the-Vote organizing, Philip Glass was also working for regime change. He was involved with three political projects during the period leading up to the 2004 U.S. presidential election, including composing music for a film about John Kerry, called *Going Up River*. Glass also donated music to use in Independent Voters of America television ads and he organized and produced a Freedom Concert for the ACLU in New York on October 4, 2004, that included Mos Def, Patti Smith, and Lou Reed.

Philip Glass currently serves on the board of directors of *Tricycle Magazine* and has performed in benefit concerts for *Tibet House* in New York City, along with Patti Smith and Laurie Anderson. In 2003, he recorded a solo piano piece titled *Dreaming Awake*, and released the CD as a benefit for Gehlek Rimpoche and Jewel Heart, a Tibetan Buddhist organization.

Philip Glass is one of the most prolific composers alive today and his dedication to exploring sound in new ways has blazed trails for many other musicians who follow in his path. His music is meditative and energetic, alerting us to awaken with a sense of freedom and peace.

▼ ▼ ▼ ▼ ▼

**John Malkin**: I want to talk to you about music, of course, but more generally about artistic expression and its influences. You have written that what has always stirred you is theater that challenges one's ideas of society and one's notions of order. What is the relationship between social change and artistic expressions like theater and music?

**Philip Glass**: I see a very direct connection. The actual content of the operas I have done expresses ideas about social change. *Satyagraha* is about social change through nonviolence. In fact, the first three operas I did—*Einstein on the Beach, Satyagraha,* and *Akhnaten* were really operas about the way the world is changed through the power of ideas. That has been true for quite a few of the works I have done since then. But it has not always been true. I have also done works which had to do not with social change, but individual transformation. Individual transformation and social change are shared ideas, in a way. They are different ends of the spectrum but ultimately the same thing. One of the things that attracted me to theater was that it was a place where the actual content of the work could address questions of social change and society.

JM: Sometimes people feel that they need to choose between social change and spiritual transformation, to choose to either address the outside world or address themselves. What do you think of that?

PG: There are only a few pieces where I have addressed both at the same time. *Satyagraha* is one example. The opera focuses on Gandhi, whose own personal development had to do with social change. But some of the other operas I have done, including the three operas devoted to scenarios based on films of Jean Cocteau, they were much more about individual transformation, you might call it spiritual if you like. Others, such as *Einstein on the Beach,* have more to do with the way the world has changed through the power of ideas, than the way an individual was changed.

JM: You have written about your opera *Akhnaten,* "*Akhnaten* changed his, and our, world through the force of his ideas and not through the force of arms." That quote seems apt to our current world situation. The violence in Iraq continues and there is a lot of fear about terrorism. I wonder what your view is on the potential to address suffering in the world today through the force of ideas rather than through the force of arms?

PG: This is a very dark moment. But I think the pendulum has already started to move in the other direction. The moment of the Republican triumph in November 2004 appears to be the moment of our greatest horror.

But I am sure that this is a moment when the reaction really begins to take hold.

What we saw in 2004 was unprecedented. We saw a large part of the country being politicized in a way they haven't been in fifty years. I don't have any doubt that we are entering into a very confrontational period right now. I think that the ideas of social order, as expressed in the extreme tradition of the Republican Party, are going to be confronted and challenged very strenuously in the next three or four years.

I am old enough to have seen the pendulum swing back and forth several times. And this is a moment when it starts to move in the other direction. I was involved in a number of projects around the November 2004 election and I had no trouble finding people to work with me on those projects. In fact, it was amazing! People who normally, or formerly, had not had any political voice at all or had any idea of how the impact of political ideas changed their lives, were extremely eager and willing to work on these issues.

JM: And it seems to you there is a new openness?

PG: Absolutely! I haven't seen anything like this since the McCarthy era and the protests around Vietnam. Four years ago, at the beginning of the Bush administration, people were tremendously passive. There was no large opposition to the war as far as I could tell. And now there is a very strong opposition, so there is a big difference.

I don't think that the November 2004 presidential election was such a great thing, but I think that this is a very interesting moment. A moment for commitment that is energizing a lot of people. I have seen this happen before. We have done this before. We are at the beginning of the movement now. I think that the next five or ten years are going to be very, very interesting.

JM: Were you politically involved in the 1950s and '60s?

PG: Well, I was a teenager then. I went to some of the Vietnam marches but I was not very ideologically driven at that time. And it wasn't long after that that I began to insinuate these ideas of social change into the work that I was doing. But, I was part of the antiwar movement, not a big part of it, but I was present when I could be. I was much more active in this November 2004 presidential election than I was forty or fifty years ago. And I think that there are many other people who are more involved now.

JM: In the 1950s, China invaded Tibet and the Buddhist nuns and monks there either escaped or were put into prison. In your 2001 introduction to Lama Yeshe's book, *Introduction to Tantra*, you wrote that, "The tragedy of Tibet turned into an unexpected and spectacular windfall for Western devotees of spiritual discipline." Tell me more about that. How has your life and music been affected by exposure to this practice?

PG: In my case it has really been the other way around. I was in touch with the Tibetan refugee community as early as 1966. I was in New York when there was only a handful of Tibetans. And now there are teaching centers all over New York. And not just New York, but all over this country. These ideas were here from the Zen teachers who came over in the forties and fifties after the Second World War and even before that.

I had the good fortune of having a very disciplined music practice and a strong teaching on this. It was part of my practice, so that when I became aware of Buddhist ideas, it wasn't a big leap. Let me put it this way, it was easier for me to attach myself to Buddhist ideas than it might have been for other people, because I already had a discipline. Do you know what I mean?

JM: Yes.

PG: The discipline of music is very, very similar to any of these spiritual practices that we are talking about. So, it facilitated, I would say, the understanding I had about them. I've written the introduction to *Taoist Qigong for Health and Vitality* and the introduction to *The Toltec Oracle* so I am not exclusively interested in the Tibetan tradition.[1] There have been other wisdom traditions that we have become more conscious of in this country in the last twenty or thirty years that I have also been interested in.

---

1 *Taoist Qigong for Health and Vitality* by Sat Chuen Hon (New York: Shambhala Publications, 2003). *The Toltec Oracle* by Victor Sanchez (Rochester, VT: Bear and Company/Inner Traditions, 2004).

**JM**: I really enjoy listening to your music. I find that it creates a certain motion and spaciousness that is almost meditative. It is meditative. I am wondering if those qualities have been enhanced through your experience with Eastern spiritual traditions?

**PG**: I really wouldn't know how to answer that question. It is very common in the arts, especially in music, for musicians and composers to talk about the emotional or spiritual depth of their music in terms of some awareness that they have. Sometimes they talk about how it is almost as if they are channeling the music. It comes from somewhere else. I would say that it is common not only in the twenty-first century, but also in the nineteenth and eighteenth century. It was very common for people to dedicate their work to the glory of God. Bruckner did it, Bach did it. Everybody did it! The joining of musical practice and spiritual practice is a very ancient thing. There are very few people that would not ascribe to that. So, when we look at it that way, we are talking about what people in our time are saying about an experience which seems to be always present.

I wouldn't say that the ideas in my music are new at all. People who consider themselves Muslims or Christians, Jewish or Buddhist all say the same thing. They all say the same thing! [Laughter] I think there is something spiritual in the experience and practice of composers and performers that is shared by many people.

**JM**: You created the piano piece *Dreaming Awake* as an offering to Gehlek Rimpoche and Jewel Heart. In the liner notes you write about how music evokes a state of mind like the state before falling asleep when we sense that we are either dreaming while awake, or awake while dreaming. Tell me more about that state of mind.

**PG**: There is an old story that after Shakyamuni Buddha achieved his enlightenment in Bodhgaya, he decided to leave and go to the Deer Park to teach. He was walking and someone came up to him, and he looked so striking to this person, his demeanor was evidently so remarkable at the time, that the person said to him, "Who are you?" He said, "I am the awakened one." In other words, he awoke from the dream. I was referring to that historical event.

But I was also referring to the common experience that many people, not

PHILIP
GLASS

65 ▶

just religious practitioners, have. A number of years ago I was talking to an old man up in Cape Breton, Nova Scotia, a man who had been a fisherman all of his life. He must have been seventy-five or eighty. We were sitting in the countryside and talking about my children. At that time my children were very young, four or five years old. And he said, "You know, it won't be long before your children will be driving up here in a big car of their own." And he looked around and said, "And all of this will be just like a dream." He was a fisherman who went to church every Sunday and that's all he knew. These are universal ideas and experiences that come to people no matter what their background. This awareness of the connection between dreaming and an awakened state comes to people who are sensitive to these ideas, no matter what tradition they come from. This was a very devout Catholic, simple man who was able to experience his life in a profound way.

JM: Buddhism is relatively new to the United States. It has been arriving from a variety of traditions and cultures and it sort of changes wherever it goes. What do you think Buddhism has to offer the United States in particular, and what do you think the United States has to offer Buddhism?

PG: I think that the second question is quite interesting. What has happened in the West, the practices, which have more or less been reserved for the monasteries, are now practiced widely by laypeople. There are people who are practicing very esoteric practices. Like you were talking about Lama Yeshe's book and the practice of Tantra. These practices aren't just done by celibate monks living in the mountains of Tibet. These are people who have jobs and families. It is quite amazing that this is happening. And if you speak to the Tibetan teachers themselves, they will tell you that they never expected this. In Tibet, these very esoteric practices are for people who have devoted their lives to them. That is not true here. Ordinary people—laypeople like you, or me, or all of the people that we know—are involved with these things. So, that is one thing the West has offered. And that is a tremendous thing, to bring those things out of such a rarified usage into a much more wide practice.

My feeling is that if we look at the current common practices in the West, it is still primarily Christianity, Judaism, and Islam. And when we look at the indigenous practices in various places, like those of the Aborigines of Australia or the indigenous people of the Americas, we can truly say that there really is no big difference in the larger spiritual ideas.

But what has happened, unfortunately, is that the practice of things that are so near at hand have become weakened a lot over the centuries. For many young people and for many modern people, these spiritual ideas don't have the power that they could have had and should have had and probably did have in the past. So, these ideas, when they come from outside, even though they are not that dissimilar, they have a freshness to them. Perhaps people might eventually rediscover things closer at home afterwards, and appreciate that. You know, the Dalai Lama often says that he considers spiritual practice in the West equally admirable and he does not encourage people to convert to Buddhism. He thought they should stick with what they knew. Of course, he doesn't know how often those ideas have been diluted. They have become rigid because the institutions themselves have over-codified them so that the experiences no longer seem available to individual people.

Hinduism, Taoism, and all of the different kinds of Buddhism seem very strong and fresh and powerful. In fact, there are meditation practices in Catholicism that could be equally powerful to Westerners when they first come across them. But many of these Judeo-Christian practices became oversimplified and practiced with a rigidity that made them suspect. That's my brief answer to a very complicated subject.

JM: I know that your composing style went through a major transformation when you first worked with Ravi Shankar in the 1960s. You were transcribing Eastern music into Western notation. I know that you struggled with this until you decided to drop the use of bar lines, in effect making "all of the notes equal," as you put it. I wonder if your exposure over the years to Eastern spirituality and philosophy has precipitated some analogous dropping of the bar lines in your life.

PG: What a nice idea! I don't know! I will have to think about it. It never occurred to me. It is a pleasant thought. What has happened to me, if dropping the bar lines means dropping the separation of traditions, that certainly has been true. I have known people from other traditions, from all of the ones we've just been talking about, and I really don't think that ultimately, if you engage with them in an energetic and a vital way, these traditions are very different. Isn't that funny? It took me a long time to come to that conclusion. And I said, "They really mean that!" Gehlek Rimpoche thinks that Christianity has a lot to offer. When I first came across that idea twenty years ago I would have dismissed the idea as naive. But I don't at all. I think he knew what he was talking about.

The differences for me have melted away. The things that are vital to me are the commitment and energy with which people approach what they do. Commitment and energy and also the stamina to carry it through.

# Phillip Glass Selected Discography

*Music With Changing Parts* – 1973 (Chatam Square)

*Music In Similar Motion/ Music In Fifths* – 1973 (Chatam Square)

*Einstein on the Beach* – 1979 (Asylum)

*North Star* – 1977 (Virgin)

*Glassworks* – 1982 (Sony)

*Mishima* – 1985 (Nonesuch Records)

*Dancepieces* – 1987 (Columbia Records)

*The Photographer* – 1983 (Columbia Records)

*Satyagraha* – 1985 (Columbia Records)

*Songs from Liquid Days* Compilation Album – 1986 (Columbia Records)

*Akhnaten* – 1987 (Columbia Records)

*Music in Twelve Parts* – 1989 (Virgin)

*Solo Piano* – 1989 (Columbia Records)

*1000 Airplanes on the Roof* – 1989 (Alliance)

*Hydrogen Jukebox* – 1993 (Nonesuch Records)

*"Low" Symphony* – 1993 (Polygram)

*Anima Mundi* Soundtrack– 1993 (Nonesuch Records)

*Music with Changing Parts* – 1994 (Nonesuch Records)

*La Belle et La Bête* – 1995 (Nonesuch Records)

*Kundun* Soundtrack– 1998 (Nonesuch Records)

*"Heroes" Symphony* – 1997 (Point)

*Koyaanisqatsi* Soundtrack – 1998 (Nonesuch Records)

*Symphony No. 2* – 1998 (Elektra/Nonesuch Records)

*Civil Wars – Rome Section* – 1999 (Nonesuch Records)

*Symphony No. 3* – 2000 (Nonesuch Records)

*Symphony No. 5* – 2000 (Nonesuch Records)

*The Hours* Soundtrack – 2002 (Nonesuch Records)

*Naqoyqatsi* Soundtrack – 2002 (Sony)

*Early Voice* – 2002 (Orange Mountain)

*Etudes for Piano* – 2003 (Orange Mountain)

*The Fog of War* Soundtrack – 2003 (Orange Mountain)

*Glassworks; In the Upper Room*– 2003 (Sony)

*Tirol Concerto* – 2003 (Orange Mountain)

# COMPASSION AND ANARCHISM

## An Interview with Utah Phillips

The new ruling party is holding the Aces,
The rest of the cards are all missing faces
I am sorry I can't know you today,
What can one say? I will not obey!
Give us your sons and give us your daughters,
No one is safe or immune from the slaughters,
How indifference makes them rage,
What can one say? I will not obey!
—from "I Will Not Obey" by Utah Phillips

IN SEPTEMBER 2004, about a year after my interview with Utah, I received a call from him: "I am heading to the East Coast soon and want to come to Santa Cruz first for a little rest and recreation—a walk at the boardwalk, hop the local, and hang out with the gang there."

Two weeks later, on a sunny Friday afternoon, a small group of us were hiding in the underbrush up the coast from Santa Cruz, listening to Utah Phillips and a friend talk about their rail travels and waiting for the local train to rev its engine and begin rolling. We hopped a couple of grainers and watched the beaches and fields of brussels sprouts go by, all the way to Watsonville.

Afterwards, walking down the street with Phillips in Santa Cruz, a few people stopped to say hello to the beloved hobo. "How does it feel to be famous?" I asked him. "Oh, I am not famous. Famous is those people who have their faces printed on the covers of those magazines at the checkout stands in grocery stores. I wouldn't want to be famous. What I am is well-known."

Utah Phillips is definitely well-known, and for a multitude of things. He is a self-proclaimed anarchist with a rich history of train-hopping, storytelling, guitar-playing, labor-organizing, and singing/songwriting. Ever since he left the military after a stint in Korea, Utah has traveled the United States offering insightful songs of social criticism to anyone who would listen. It didn't take long for the crowds to gather.

Phillips was born with the name Bruce Phillips in Cleveland, Ohio in 1939. His father, Edwin, was a communist. His mother worked with the CIO (Congress of Industrial Organizations) before it merged with the AFL and his father was a communist youth organizer. His parents divorced when he was five and Phillips' mother remarried Sid Cohen, the manager of the Hippodrome Theatre, the last of the old vaudeville houses in Cleveland. Around this time he learned to play the ukulele from a Japanese-Hawaiian man who was a counselor at the Jewish youth camp he attended.

In 1947, Phillips moved to Salt Lake City, Utah with his mother and stepfather. He wandered away so often that, as he has put it, his "mother started wrapping his lunch in a road map." Later he went to work in Yellowstone National Park, where some of the older road crew workers taught him how to turn his Hawaiian slack-key ukulele chords into guitar chords. It was at Yellowstone that he picked up "Utah" as his nickname.

Phillips joined the military and was sent to Korea, where he helped to found a band, the Rice Paddy Ramblers. He had an encounter with a local Korean man that woke him to the destruction and violence that he was participating in. Philliips decided to leave the military and went to a place called the Korea House in Seoul, where he was hidden for three weeks before leaving the country behind. It was during his last weeks in Korea that Phillips attended a performance at the Aiwa Women's University by vocalist Marion Anderson, who sang "Oh Freedom" and "Nobody Knows the Trouble I've Seen." He was reminded of the racism that he'd witnessed when Anderson had performed years before at his stepfather's theater and had been refused entry to the local hotel because she was black.

After returning to the United States, Phillips cruised the country via freight trains for two years, making up songs. He headed for Salt Lake City after he discovered a place that offered free food and clothing. It would be a life-changing journey. It was at the Joe Hill House for Transients and Migrants in Salt Lake City that Phillips befriended Ammon Hennacy, who described himself as a "Catholic-anarchist-pacifist draft-dodger of two world wars, tax-refuser, vegetarian, wise-guy, and one-man revolution in America." Hennacy was a part of the Catholic Worker movement that had been started by Catholic anarchists Dorothy Day and Peter Maurin in the 1930s. The houses provided hospitality, soup kitchens, and opportunities for direct actions opposing war and exploitation. Phillips' political awakening was accelerated during the eight years that he spent at the Joe Hill House. Hennacy taught him about anarchism ("An anarchist is anybody who doesn't need a cop to tell him what to do"), nonviolence ("Force is the weapon of the weak"), and pacifism ("It's not just giving up guns and knives and clubs and fists and angry words, but giving up the weapons of privilege, and going into the world completely unarmed").

Phillips continued to play guitar, write songs, and tell stories at bars and cafes. In 1960, he was approached by Kenneth S. Goldstein, a folklorist from the University of Pennsylvania, who had traveled to Utah for a folklore conference. Goldstein overheard Phillips singing on his front porch and invited him to record what became his first album, *No One Knows Me*. This recording was done at the local university on a rented tape recorder.

Phillips has long combined social change and music to serve his desire to contribute to positive change. One of his early songs was "Enola Gay," about the United States' nuclear bombing of Japan. His lyrics and stories have often addressed issues of poverty, war, and self-determination, but with a robust sense of humor.

In the 1960s, Phillips volunteered for Fair Play for Cuba, helped to reform housing laws in Utah, and worked for the Migrant Council. In 1968, he ran for U.S. Senate as a Peace and Freedom Party candidate. After his run for office, he found himself jobless. Phillips left Utah in November of 1969 in an old VW Bus with seventy-five dollars in his pocket. Phillips currently lives in Nevada City, California.

Phillips's storytelling has been compared to that of Mark Twain and Will Rogers and he has received numerous awards, including the 1989 Kate Wolf Memorial Award from the North American Folk Music and Dance Alliance, the 1997 Lifetime Service to Labor Award from the American Federation of Musicians, Travelling Musicians Local 1000, and the 1997 NAIRD (National Association of Independent Record Distributors) Award for best traditional recording, with Rosalie Sorrels.

Though he officially retired in 1996, after a heart condition slowed down his pace of 120 shows a year, he still performs many benefit shows. Recently

Phillips brought his voice to a massive protest at the School of the Americas in Fort Benning, Georgia, the U.S. government's institution that has trained hundreds of foreign military personnel in techniques of torture and violence.

Utah Phillips is always on the lookout for a story to learn or a cause to support. When I have spent time with him—exchanging the Jewish stories that we grew up hearing or hopping on a moving freight train—I am reminded of how mythologist Joseph Campbell distilled into one sentence the main teaching of all of the world's spiritual traditions: "Don't do anything that isn't play." My hope is that Utah Phillips will be playing for years and years to come.

▼ ▼ ▼ ▼ ▼

**John Malkin**: You are such a storyteller in your songs. Tell me a little more about that and some of the stories you grew up with.

**Utah Phillips**: I was born in Cleveland, Ohio. My mother and father divorced when I was about five. My father was a communist and a youth organizer. He sold the *Daily Worker* on the streets. My mother had worked briefly for the CIO, the Congress of Industrial Organizations. They were both radicals.

At one point there was a Tenant Union strike, near as I can tell. Everybody was living in a tent including my older brother, one year older than me. No future for two small children, two infants, you know. So, my mother left my dad and she became a fashion model. What is a single woman with two children to do? She had been a beauty pageant winner in high school and became a fashion model for Higbee Brothers in Cleveland, walking the runway upstairs at the top in the lunchroom. With a dressing room backstage. My brother and I would be in the dressing room backstage.

I haven't thought about this in years but it was beautiful. My brother and I would sneak away—two little kids—and we would get on the elevator and go all the way down to the basement of Terminal Towers where the big trains came in. The big steam passenger locals would come in and I would go down to the head end, where the engine and the driver were. These things had enormous engines. A grown person couldn't touch the top of those drivers. Just before it was going to start, the engineer yelled, "Start," and then I would become enveloped in this cloud of warm steam. I couldn't see anything at all. It was marvelous, like being in a fog bank.

My stepfather, Sid Cohen, was a young Jewish businessman. All these young guys would go and have lunch at the roof of the Higbee Brothers, to watch the models. He fell in love with my mother and courted her off of the runway. He was the son of immigrant Jews. His father was named Simon Bialibjetsky, but his name was Cohen. Why? Well, the same old story. When he immigrated, the official said, "I can't spell your name. What is your tribe?" He answered: "Cohen." So, that became his name. For him just out of college to marry a *shiksa* with two children, and move us into the old Jewish neighborhood next door to his father was quite a commitment. There we were. That is where I spent the first twelve years of my life, and it was a place full of juice and full of life. There were people on the porches in the summer, talking and playing Yiddish records. There were still hand-cranked Victrolas. During the Second World War, when there was gas rationing, there were still horses in the street. The ragman, the coal scowl, the vegetable seller just never did give up the horses. Why bother if you are going to ration gasoline? It was just an exciting place to grow up.

My grandfather Simon was Orthodox. My grandmother Lily wasn't. I don't know quite what Lily was. She was younger than Simon. Simon would sit at the end of the hall. My first memory of him was that he had cataracts or some other eye problem and the doctor said, "If you sit at the end of the hall..." and he gave him a prism, "and you put something at the other end of the hall..."—in this case it was some dried flowers in a pot—"and you hold that prism up to your eyes and practice bringing the images together, you won't have to have an eye operation." So every morning, on rising, Simon was at the end of the hall—this tiny man, very old—with a prism focusing on those dried flowers. And while he was there, my mother would come across, where Lily was, my grandmother, and together they would fry up bacon in the kitchen and eat it quickly before Simon came in.

One of my first memories as a little kid, five or six years old, was to come across from the house next door, wondering where my mother was, and find in the dead of Winter, my grandmother Lily and my mother standing in the kitchen flapping their aprons to get the bacon smoke out the windows before Simon came in. The place is freezing. [Laughter]

My memories of Simon are in the living room of that house, during the

Second World War, with his ear glued to the curtain on the front of the Atwater-Kent, the big stand up radio. All of those old radios had a short-wave band and he was there with his ear right up against it. He was hard of hearing and he was turning the dial—whiiirree—just trying to pick up any news about what was happening in Europe, because his whole family was there. He sold home heating oil and spent most of the money he had saved for retirement trying to get people out of Poland. It didn't succeed at all. When he retired, he had very little because he had given it up. As a child watching him, I didn't understand then what he was doing.

Once there was a terrible storm. Lightning came through the front room window, set the carpet on fire right at my grandfather's feet and he did not pull his ear away from that radio! My grandmother came in and poured water on the rug, from the kitchen. That is how he was.

It was a whole different life there, because then we moved to Utah to an all-Mormon town! It was 1947 and that was the Centennial of the Mormon Pioneer Trek when Jim Bridger had brought Brigham Young to the valley. Well, the whole town was full of Mormon pioneer stuff. What do I know? Nobody explained this to me, why these people are behaving like this.

The boys in our neighborhood were so snotty and so quiet. It was so different than with Simon. Nobody was yelling. No alleys to run through. If you're going to grow up civilized, you have got to have alleys to run through, for crying out loud. Where are the alleys? It was hard for me to get used to the idea of being in Salt Lake City.

Fortunately, my mother sent me to the Boy Scouts when I got old enough. The troop meetings took place at the Mormon Wards. It is like a parish. Then my mother discovered that they wouldn't let black kids into the Boy Scouts. So, she pulled us out. A lot of other parents did the same thing. There was a big Jewish community in Salt Lake, two of them, Reformed and Orthodox, and had been for years. So, parents formed a Camp Bet Yeledim, a Jewish youth camp. We had our own meetings. I did acquire a Jewish peer group. They were spread out all over the city, but not in the neighborhood. We had a Camp Yeledim. *Yeledim*—children in Hebrew. The Jewish youth camp met in the summers at the Methodist College. My camp counselor was a Japanese-Hawaiian, Tetsuo Okada, who managed a French bakery called "Pinos." It was a very eclectic environment. He was the one who taught me to play the ukulele and the first one to start teaching me to play the guitar. He gave me the guitar and he showed me how to play it. Two years later I was up in Yellowstone working in a restaurant kitchen and these guys on the road crews, these old drunks who knew a lot of old Jimmy Rogers songs heard me playing and said, "What is that?"

See, Tetsuo thought the guitar was always tuned in a Mauna Loa G slack-key. So the first guitar I learned in Utah was slack-key Hawaiian music. The Yellowstone crew guys showed me how I could re-tune the guitar so that I could play civilized gringo music. That is when I started writing songs and listening to what they were singing. I guess that is how those two things come together.

JM: I am curious how Judaism and socialism and communism helped to shape who you have become and the sort of work that you do and the stories that you tell. Also, when did you first encounter anarchism?

UP: I think I was always aware, through my mother and through Leo Huber-man's book, *We, the People*. It was a radical history of the American people and it was blacklisted.

When I would come home from school, with my history book and with a little one-page paper about history, if I got a passing grade, my mother would tear it up and say I failed. She would give me the Huberman book and say, "Here. Write out of this." I would take that to school and they would say, "This isn't acceptable," and she'd say, "Congratulations." So, I have always known through her, even though she wasn't raised Jewish, that the backbone of American radicalism was the Jewish bunds.

The bunds were organizations of Jewish immigrant laborers. The Bismarck order had expelled a lot of the Jewish socialists from Europe and they came to Chicago and formed the Butcher's and Baker's Unions and became a key part of the backbone of the labor movement. That has always been part of my consciousness.

The strongest movement among Jews in the 1890s was the anarchist move-ment. There was a wonderful movie called *The Jewish Anarchists*. The tragedy of that long radical Jewish tradition here in this country is that after the Holocaust, when Britain finally gave Palestine to the Zionists and Churchill's dream came true, it became very difficult to be a Jew in this country and not be a Zionist. That undermined Jewish radicalism very, very seriously.

To talk about Palestinian liberation, to talk about a secular state, to talk about Israel as a multi-ethnic, secular democracy and not a religious state—that is the pickle that Jewish radicals are in now. I am glad that a lot of Jews have organized, such as the Middle East Children's Alliance that is doing marvelous work, a lot of it by Jewish radicals.

I have always thought that there should be a different word than "anarchy." I didn't grow up with that word. The word has been so stigmatized ever since the Haymarket in 1886 when they began to characterize anarchists as bomb-throwers and extremely violent people. "Anarchos" means without a ruler, but we need to be talking about *self-rule*. We are talking about becoming your own government. The President of the United States of You! And you can do it better and cheaper than they can. What can we call this self-government? Let's come up with a different word that really describes what we're up to.

When I got back from Korea, I just roamed around. I got drunk a lot and didn't know if I could live in the country anymore. I was working in a warehouse in Salt Lake. Ammon Hennacy came in with one of the Catholic Worker people and opened the Joe Hill House, named for the great Wobblie song maker. And I worked out there for eight years. Ammon Hennacy was a Catholic-anarchist-pacifist draft-dodger of two world wars, tax-refuser, vegetarian, wise-guy, and one-man revolution in America. That's what he called himself. He took me over, dried me out on a marathon picket line and convinced me that I loved the country. He didn't tell me what to do. He taught by example. He lived and behaved a certain way and I saw that this man was happy and that this man was productive. This man was able to tell himself what to do. He didn't need somebody to tell him what to do. He said, "An anarchist is anybody who don't need a cop to tell him what to do."

There are all kind of cops in the world: teachers, preachers, parents—anybody who feels they have the right and ability to tell you what to do is some kind of cop. If you assert your right and your ability to make just and humane decisions and when you blow it, you look at it as an opportunity to change and you do change, then you're starting to become an anarchist.

Ammon came to me one day and he said, "You know, all we ever wanted to do was create voluntary combinations among ourselves." We want to create combinations that serve our needs as we define them and not as they are defined for us. We need to have combinations that are not culturally compelled. We have grown up in a world of cultural compulsion.

Once Ammon said to me, "You're wearing socks." I said, "Yeah." He said, "They're both the same color." I said, "Yeah." He said, "Why? Why are your socks the same color? Did you choose that when you took them out of the drawer in the morning?" I said, "No." He said, "That's cultural compulsion and it hits you a thousand times a day and you don't even know that it's hitting you." You have to sit down with a notebook and take a whole day apart and see how much of your behavior is really compulsive and how much is really voluntary.

So, having dealt with a cultural compulsion, you want to start building combinations with other people and try to get the work of the world done. Ammon said, "If you and I can agree to do our share of our work in the world, around here, if you and I can agree to take only what we need and put back what we can, if you and I can agree to care for the afflicted and if you and I can agree not to hurt anybody, then we can begin to form that voluntary combination and start to get the work of the world done without the boss and without the State."

JM: You're saying that part of anarchism is compassion and nonviolence and yet a common view now of anarchism is that it is synonymous with violence and chaos.

UP: Yes. The president and other politicians say they can't do anything radical because it would be anarchy. To them, anarchy equals chaos. Well, anarchists have got to be the best organized people in the world. If you're going to become your own government, you've got to be good at organizing. If you are going to organize voluntary combinations, cooperatives, and collectives you're going to have to be well-organized.

The problem is that there are too many people calling themselves anarchists who act out a lot. They say, "You can't tell me what to do. If anybody gets in my way, I will knock them down." That is a blueprint for self-destruction. Part of our task is not just to talk to people about what anarchy is and who anarchists are, but to talk to the nihilists and try to wean them from it back to anarchy. Compassion is a really big part of that. By compassion I mean nonviolence! I mean, good heavens. The government can escalate from a cop with a handgun up to a hydrogen bomb and everything in between. The man owns that game and he is always saying, "Come up that road with me," you know? If you give in, you are done for. Either that or, if you win, then you've got the guns now and you start pushing people around. The State recreates itself. We have to take another road, a road he doesn't own, a road he doesn't understand. It's the road of nonviolence. Nonviolence is not just a tactic or a strategy, it is a practical necessity.

JM: One criticism of nonviolent activists in North America is that they are privileged to have the leisure and time to actually be experimenting with nonviolence when there are people in other parts of the world who don't have that privilege and need to take up arms. What do you think of that? Also, we were talking earlier about how the notion of revolution has changed, that the idea of abrupt overthrow of power structures has not worked, and that by taking over and owning the weapons of those in power, one is not really in a place of power anyway.

UP: Lenin said that revolution consumes its own children. Why? Because the people who go through the experience of revolution, the horror, the degradation, and the need to kill render themselves unfit to govern people. The post-revolutionary government is often the most violent. I think we witness that in most any revolution. I can't tell people what to do. If you want a violent revolution, have a revolution, but spare me no illusions about this. We need to do something else besides become the State we are fighting against.

JM: What is your impression of the Zapatistas in Chiapas, Mexico, and their spokesperson, Subcomandante Marcos?

UP: Global revolution is being redefined by Subcomandante Marcos. The Zapatistas bring a whole new set of ideas about populist organizing. They exemplify what Che Guevara said about revolution: "At the risk of seeming absurd, the true revolutionary is moved by profound feelings of love." Doesn't that hit you like a ton of bricks?

How do you deal with complex economic issues through what I am talking about? I don't know. I have no post-revolutionary analysis. It is not up to me to figure that out or impose it on anybody. I simply want to get together with people who feel and who want to live their freedom without hurting other people and be the architects of their own lives.

JM: In the liner notes for one of the CDs you've done with Ani DiFranco, *The Past Didn't Go Anywhere*, you wrote, "Buddha's students asked him, 'Are you a saint?' He said, 'No.' After awhile they asked him, 'Are you an angel?' He said, 'No.' 'Then what are you?' they asked. The Buddha replied, 'I am awake.'"

UP: Yes. Wake up! That's all. Just get out of yourself. Turn your eyes outward, beat the streets, and ask questions. That is a wonderful thing to do. Most of the time, the only questions people ever get asked is, "How come you're late?" or "How soon can you get it out?" They go through their whole lives like that. People can be married forty years and watch the same television news broadcasts and never turn to each other and say, "Hey honey, what do you really feel about that?" People have these thoughts and feelings and ideas, opinions all ganged up inside and nobody ever asks about it. You start asking questions about all of that and of course, first off, they're suspicious, "Are you trying to sell me something?" But once you convince them that you really want to hear them, they unburden. Everything starts to flow out. Just asking questions and following my nose, that's my university.

We are each born with four gifts. First, we have the gift of curiosity, which I never gave up. And the second gift is the gift of memory. The third gift is our capacity for logic. How do you organize the flow of stuff coming through? What are the patterns? What is the geometry of this? And the final gift is our ability to endow everything with a profound sense of play. While our school system and society try to hammer these gifts out of us, I have never given these things up and I am very happy with my life.

JM: You are a great storyteller. Originally television was being sold as the great instrument for storytelling. What happened?

UP: It has turned out a great many stories. Madison Avenue has studied the psychology of story telling and learned to tell stories. But they use them to sell products. They have learned how to jerk us around. The key building block to a nonviolent future and a nonviolent family and community is to turn the goddamned thing off. In one final fit of violence—pick your TV up and throw it out in the middle of the street and then learn to live in peace with other people! Open your mouths, sounds will ensue. Arrange them in a cogent form: subject, verb, predicate. Talk to each other, by God! It will be a blessed relief. Get rid of those ugly, exploited images that are hammered into you by highly manipulative people. One of the key seeds of peace is getting rid of the television set.

There is an old story from a Peace Corps fellow in Africa who left a TV set behind when the Peace Corps left the village he was staying in. When the fellow went back five years later, the villagers weren't watching the TV. He asked one of the village leaders, "Why aren't you watching the television?" And the leader said, "Because we have a storyteller here." The Peace Corps fellow asked, "But doesn't the TV know more stories than your storyteller?" And the villager said, "Yes, it does know more stories than our storyteller, but the storyteller knows me." It's all of the difference in the world.

Your parents, grandparents, your neighbors all have a story. What is the substance of their life? I don't mean their opinions about politics and stuff they read in the paper or pick up off of CNN or Fox, but what is the truth of their lives? What is the truth of your job, of your tools, of your kin, of your neighborhood? So, get busy folks and start asking real questions. Not rhetorical questions. Not questions where you think you already know the answer, but real questions that turn your curiosity loose. Don't give up learning.

JM: The Dalai Lama has said that his religion is kindness. What is your religion?

UP: It was one of the English naturalists whose dying words were, "Try to be a little kinder." Lovely. Sometimes it is extremely difficult to follow these words, but I try to reach for the best in everybody. Always dealing with the best, and dealing with the worst only when you have to, when you are driven to it. When I would criticize a cop, Ammon would say, "He is a good man doing a bad job." He'd say, "There are no bad people. There are good people doing terrible jobs and doing terrible things."

When you think that way, you lay down an awfully heavy burden. Once you've dropped that, you can think more clearly. You can see more clearly and act more constructively. We need to build, not destroy. So much revolution destroys what the workers have built. We don't want to destroy what people who have led true lives have built—the buildings, this library. We can't tear down our own stuff.

JM: What is your impression of the attacks of September 11, 2001, and the U.S. reaction?

UP: The country has fallen into the hands of assholes and I don't need to be told again and again and again that they are assholes. I know that they are assholes. It is just obvious! So, how do you deal with chronic, insipient ass-holery? How do you deal with the corporatization of the executive branch of the government? The government is behaving more and more like a corporation and corporations are anti-democratic organizations. How do you deal with it? Well, you resist.

An old organizer I knew named Campbell once said, "Freedom is something you assume and then you wait for somebody to try to take it away from you. The degree to which you resist is the degree to which you are free." By demonstrating in cities all over the country people are trying to punch through to mass media and show that support for war is super thin. The numbers of people protesting will grow and grow and grow. They will have to listen to us.

During the first Gulf war, an air raid shelter in Iraq was hit by a U.S. missile. There were over four hundred families in there and the missile bored right through all the concrete and killed everybody inside. This year, families of people killed at the World Trade Center stood with Iraqis who had lost their relatives in the wreckage of that air raid shelter and they held a common prayer service. That is the best face of anarchy. It is through that kind of action that we can win.

We can't lose heart. There is a massive amount of force and a massive amount of destruction that looms on the horizon, but we can beat it. We can win. I can't say that too often. The biggest act of repression that happened in this country was the Palmer Raids of 1919 that came out of the Espionage Act passed during the First World War. Thousands and thousands of people were put in jail. People being lynched and hung from the telephone poles because they had German last names. The Sedition Acts were far worse than anything we are experiencing now. They were far worse than the Patriot Act and we still came out of it. We came out of the Great Depression, grinding economic degradation and the beginning of political repression, with social security, with workman's compensation, and the minimum wage because organized workers rammed it down the government's throat. Roosevelt just stood out of the way.

McCarthyism, the effort to destroy the labor movement, and the beginning of the Cold War, make what is happening now look tame. And we came out of all that at the end of the 1950s with a victorious Civil Rights movement. Recently, I was driving and speeding through Mississippi and I was stopped and issued a citation by a black highway patrolman. I said, "Hey, we won!" We created an antiwar movement that, according to Richard Nixon, prevented him from using nuclear weapons on North Vietnam. And we are going to come out of this this time as well. Come on. We have done it before. If you think we can't do it; if you think you have to move to Canada; if you think you have to throw in the towel; if you think that it is just hopeless; then you're turning your back on all those people who went to jail during the Palmer Raids, all of those people who gave us social security and went to the wall for it, and all of those people who got beat up in Mississippi for voter registration. You're betraying and turning your back on all of those people and wouldn't you feel awful if you did leave the country and we came out of this even better, and you had to come back? Keep the faith, brothers and sisters, keep the faith. That is your sermon for today.

JM: What role do radio and media play in creating social change?

UP: Free radio is the kind of radio we want. These are the people's airwaves and we have to assert our right to them, just as we have to hang on to the national parks, the public schools, and the postal service. All of the things that we own together are under such violent assault by a handful of maladjusted people who think that everything needs to be owned and everything needs to make money for somebody.

Capitalism has no use for government now except to deregulate, privatize everything that we own, provide tax relief to the wealthy, and create an army paid for by its citizens and used to enforce corporate interests globally. This is what they are trying to get away with in Iraq right now. The frontline, the trenches of that defense, are right here in little rooms with broadcast equipment across the country. This is our people's voice.

JM: One way that you've resisted the government is by not paying taxes. Tell me about your experience with war tax resistance.

UP: I stopped paying taxes after what I saw in Korea. I have dug up landmines and seen how people are being killed by landmines around the world. I don't want to pay for landmines. I don't want to pay for smart bombs dropped by dumb people. Around forty years ago, I wrote the government a letter that said, "Look, there are some things you people are doing that I agree with. I like the national parks, so if you'll tell me where I can send my money and let me earmark it the way we do with the United Way, I will be happy to do it." And the letter I got back said, "If every tax payer asked for this service, pretty soon there wouldn't be any government." Cool! So, they know where I am and they know where to come and get me. I don't have much of anything they can take away. They can't take away the freedom in my head. My thoughts are free. I don't feel I am doing anything wrong. I am doing things right.

Most of my work in life, part of the money that I have made, I have given away to things I believe in. About a quarter of my time on the stage are benefits for things I believe in. I write it down so I know where every penny went. Another way of doing this is getting together with other people and taking the money that you would pay in taxes and putting it into an alternative fund. Then your community could submit proposals for how the money should be used and distributed. Put what you would normally pay in taxes to people who spend it on bombs and guns and put it to work in your community in combination with other people, and make it a better community.

JM: On your website it says, "Mors Ante Servitium"—death before employment.

UP: That's a tramp aphorism that used to be embroidered on the outside of the bedroll of Dawdlin' Bill, a great tramp up there in Montana. He was a very slow man. He took his time with whatever he was doing and he was good on the trains.

JM: Are you still riding the rails?

UP: I have congestive heart failure, which makes it very difficult. I miss the trains with a deep passion. I always rode alone because I wanted to be alone during that period of my life. But there is a unique kind of freedom, being in a clean and empty grainer. It is almost mystical. Nobody can get you. There is no phone, no fax, no cop. You are underway. The engineer, the train, is going someplace and you don't know where. The engineer is like God. He doesn't know you're there and you are not aware of his intentions. It is a unique kind of freedom. Anybody who wants that freedom can have it. You can be absolutely free. But there is a serious price to pay for it, if you want it. Cold. Alone. Sick. Lonely. Nobody looking out for you except yourself. But, you can be free.

JM: In 1995, you went to the doctor and found out you'd had a heart attack.

UP: He told me that I had had a heart attack and I said, "No, I didn't." And he said, "Yes, you did." He looked on the angiogram, on the TV screen and said, "See, there's a whole part of your heart that doesn't work anymore." We call that a silent heart attack. He said, "It must've been a lousy day, you missed a heart attack." It's called congestive heart failure. When my cardiologist first started examining me, he asked, "What do you do for a living?" So, I described what I do, town for town, thirty-three years, singing songs and stuff. He said, "You mean you abandon yourself to the judgment of strangers serially? No wonder you had a heart attack!" No sane person would do that! He understood right away. I never thought of it that way, but he was absolutely right. He told me that I had to stop touring. I was on my way to a long tour, in through Montana and up to Calgary and that meant going over a number of seven thousand–foot passes, and that is bad for people with congestive heart failure, at least at that stage where I was. He said, "You do this tour and you're not going to come back." So, I cancelled it. For a while I cancelled everything.

I would go out and tour and do my work, but then I'd come home and I'd sit on the couch for weeks and be barely vegetating. My wife thought I was depressed. But, it turned out I was just running out of the adrenalin that had been keeping me going. My cardiologist said, "The heart attack was probably the result of dosing yourself on adrenalin before you went on stage." I backed into this trade. This wasn't a trade of choice. I did it because I was on a black-list of "undesirables" in Utah and had to find work. I am a worried, frightened performer. He said, "You've hammered your heart with adrenalin for thirty years and now you're seeing the results."

JM: Can you describe how you deal with fear?

UP: I am brave to the point of madness. Fear. I deal with fear partly through avoidance. As an old habit, I turn my back and walk away from it. I guess my deepest fear is my own capacity for violence. My own capacity for rage. And I have waking fantasies of terrible violence. I'm a pacifist because I have to be, the way an alcoholic has to stop drinking.

During the Gulf War, I was knocked off a stool in a bus stop and cafe in Idaho Falls. I was taking the buses and trains because my car doesn't run on blood. A guy saw my peace button and knocked me off my stool. You find out if you're a pacifist somewhere on the way to the floor. I picked myself up and I shook his hand and said, "I am sorry that you feel that way" and I got on the bus and left. I felt really good about doing that instead of exploding, which I would have done in years past.

My greatest fears are things that I harbor inside myself. For that reason, I've moved through the world a lot, trying to move away from the source of the fear and the source of the pain and not being able to do so. The minute I stopped doing that, the minute I stood still, everything I was running from banged into my ass. And that is when I find my courage. Ammon Hennacy said, "Courage is the principal virtue because without it you can't practice any of the others."

So, I found my courage, and I was able to learn how to live in one place and live with myself. There are still dark spots, mostly about my family and things from when I was very young. I'll never really get at those. Once I found my courage and confronted myself, I really decided that there are some things that are not going to change. I can't change them. So I put them on the shelf as artifacts—that is what I am doing these days.

JM: You've written, "The stories I tell don't just come out of my own life. Many of them come to me from my elders. I strain to hear them through the roar of my own ego, my own needs and desires. But when I become quiet and open to the thoughts and feelings of my elders, I learn that my life story deepens, grows richer, by taking in the stories of those who have led extraordinary lives, lives that can never be lived again." Tell me about that process of quieting and listening to others and asking questions.

UP: I guess the first elder I ever paid any attention to was when I ran away from Salt Lake to the Navajo Indian reservation, on the edge of the San Juan River. I hid way out in the desert at Saint Christopher's Mission of the Navajo. It was a red sandstone cloister, up against the cliffs, that had been there for years and years. There was nothing but desert around, and the San Juan River, and Father Baxter Liebler. He wore the Navajo bun, even had the full cassock, and was from the Good Shepherd Episcopalian Church in New Jersey. He was well-born and had a lot of money but got the call and instead of taking a mule and the Bible into the desert, went to Cornell University and studied Navajo language and religion. Then he went into the desert, and he built his own church with his own hands. He did two song masses a day with Navajo and Zuni medicine chants for the music instead of the plainsong. I can still sing some of those.

I remember looking into his crowded little room in the little stone cloister of Father Liebler's church and seeing a couple of rusty fencing foils. Fencing was the only sport I ever took up. And I said to Father Liebler, "Where'd you get those?" He took them out and said, "Do you fence?" The old man hadn't picked those up for twenty-five years. But we started fencing in the yard, with the Navajo kids running around there. They were saying, "What the hell is it?" We kept backing each other up. He touched me again and again—he was fast! Finally I was exhausted and I said, "Where did you learn how to do that?" He said, "Well, I got my Latin and Greek at the Sorbonne in Paris, living in a garret, but there was no place to take a bath. The only way I could wash was by joining the gymnasium. In order to join the gymnasium, you had to take a class." So, he took fencing. Father Liebler was the first elder who I really listened to and paid attention to. I was married for the first time in his church.

After I left the reservation, I went back to Salt Lake and got a job in the warehouse at the Western Movie Supply. My boss there was an old man named Earl Lyman who was the grandson of Amassa M. Lyman, one of the original apostles of the Mormon Church during the pioneer trek. Earl Lyman liked to tell stories about the old Mormon days. He would come back to the big long table with a roll of butcher paper where I wrapped parcels for the trucks to come and carry things away.

He would climb up on my packing desk and lean his back up against the butcher paper and just talk. It didn't take me long to realize that as long as he was lying there, I couldn't work. So, I would go to the library after work and look up books of Mormon history and then come in the morning and ask him questions. "What about the Mount Meadows? The Morrisites? What about the Gadianton Robbers?" He'd hoist himself up there and start yarning and I couldn't work. That is where I learned about storytelling as a part of work avoidance.

JM: Did you ever meet Dorothy Day?

UP: I met Dorothy Day in New York City when I first left Utah. I took Ammon's greeting to her. They were lovely people. Ammon Hennacy, my third elder teacher, loved Dorothy with a deep animal passion and she loved him with a great spiritual passion. And they used to say, in the Catholic Worker about them, "the horniest of men meets the holiest of women." I am probably telling tales out of school. I probably shouldn't even talk about this stuff.

Dorothy Day sent Ammon west. She said, "Get out of here and go to Utah!" Utah is really off the edge of the world, but Ammon started the Joe Hill Hospitality House there. Ammon sent me back to talk to Dorothy and she very kindly gave me a wonderful first edition of Peter Maurin's *The Green Revolution*.[2] She asked me what I was doing in the East and I said, "Well, I've been blacklisted in Utah and I want to try and make a living singing songs and telling stories on the stage." She said, "Just remember that fame corrupts the house of the soul." That has been my guiding light ever since. I may be well-known, but fame was never my intention.

Fame isolates you and I don't want to be separated from the people who I'm with, who I'm learning from, and who I'm singing to. I want to be treated like a good carpenter, a good plumber, or a good electrician. I just want to

2 Fresno, CA: Academy Guild Press, 1961.

be treated as an honest American worker, plying my trade. When I am at home, we put the garbage out on Monday and the garbage man takes it away. I turn on the tap and water comes out. It is clear, clean water. I flush the toilet and the waste goes away. These things happen because there are people working at the sewage treatment plant, at the water purification plant, and at the garbage dump. My life would be miserable if those people didn't do those things and do them well. Why isn't anybody out asking for the garbage man's autograph? Next time you have a chance, go to your mail person and say, "Can I have your autograph?" Nobody should have any kind of elevated position or "power" that goes with that. Dorothy Day knew the value of being powerless but not motionless.

That's why I stay out of politics. "Poly" is Greek for many and "ticks" are blood-sucking insects. I think that anybody who aspires to a position of power, where they own and have the ability to use all of those nuclear weapons, is insane to begin with. I will stay away from it. I vote. Ammon Hennacy never went to the ballot box. Ammon said that his body was his ballot. An old friend once asked me, "When two people are having a fight, which one pulls the knife first?" The losing one, of course. Force is the weapon of the weak.

My friends, we need each other. Joseph Campbell, late in his life, said, "All we ever want is to be completely human and in each other's company." So let's take this opportunity. All you good people, all you people who believe in justice, kindness, humanity, and peace, let's get shoulder to shoulder and rub hands, stare each other in the eye. Let's talk together. Let's be completely human and for God's sake, let's be in each other's company.

# Utah Phillips Selected Discography

*El Capitan* – 1969 (Philo Records)
*Good Though* – 1973 (Philo Records)
*All Used Up: A Scrapbook* – 1975 (Philo Records)
*We Have Fed You All For a Thousand Years* – 1984 (Philo Records)
*Don't Mourn – Organize!* Compilation Album – 1990 (Smithsonian Folkways)
*I've Got To Know* – 1991 (Alcazar)
*The Past Didn't Go Anywhere* with Ani DiFranco – 1996 (Righteous Babe)
*Long Memory* with Rosalie Sorrels – 1996 (Red House)
*Loafer's Glory* with Mark Ross – 1997 (Red House)
*Telling Takes Me Home* – 1997 (Philo Records)
*Fellow Workers* with Ani DiFranco – 1999 (Righteous Babe)
*Moscow Hold & Other Stories* – 1999 (Red House)

# DEDICATION

Well I climbed the seven summits and I swam the seven seas

But the road I must travel, its end I cannot see.

Well I fought in the jungles and I fought in the streets

But the road I must travel, its end I cannot see.

I once had a reason, don't know what it could be,

But the road I must travel, its end I cannot see

Well I sang to myself that I want to be free

But the road I must travel, its end I cannot see.

—from "The Road I Must Travel" by The Nightwatchman (Tom Morello)

On March 21, 2003, the U.S. government went to war in Iraq. President George W. Bush promised that the bombing of Baghdad would bring "shock and awe" to the Iraqi people and bring the government of Iraq into submission. I was in San Francisco that night, to see Tom Morello's band, Audioslave.

After the show, Tom Morello and Chris Cornell, Audioslave's lead singer, told me that they were disappointed by the war and that they'd hoped that the massive worldwide protests for peace would have dissuaded the U.S. government from such action. On stage that night at the Warfield, a hand-made sign read, "How many Iraqis per gallon?" and Cornell sang an acoustic version of "What's So Funny about Peace, Love, and Understanding?"

Tom Morello is well-acquainted with political protest. His mother, Mary Morello, is the founder of Parents for Rock and Rap, an anti-censorship organization. His father, whom he didn't meet until later in his life, was a guerrilla in the Mau Mau uprising that helped free Kenya from British rule. While going to preschool in Libertyville, Illinois a little white girl called him "nigger." When he asked his mother what the word meant, she told him about the history of racial conflicts in America and about Malcolm X. When the little girl made the same remarks the next day, Tom responded with, "Shut up, whitey!" and then punched her in the face.

Morello was inspired to learn guitar after listening to a recording of the Sex Pistols. In high school, he formed a band with bassist Adam Jones, who later became the guitarist for Tool. The name of their band, the Electric Sheep, was a name taken from the title of Philip K. Dick's novel, *Do Androids Dream of Electric Sheep?*, which was made into the film *Blade Runner.*

After graduating from Harvard University in social studies, Morello went to Los Angeles with the intention of forming a rock band. He also taught guitar lessons and worked as a secretary for Senator Alan Cranston. He was fired from the job when he confronted a constituent over the phone who complained that "colored people" were moving into her neighborhood. He played in several bands before forming a punk rock band called Lock Up, at which time he met Brad Wilk. Morello and Wilk then formed Rage Against the Machine in 1991, with vocalist Zack de la Rocha and bassist Tim Commerford.

Their first show was in the living room of a friend's house in Huntington Beach, California. They then produced a twelve-song demo tape that sold 5,000 copies. After playing the Lollapalooza II Tour at Irvine Meadows, California, they were signed to Epic Records. Their first European tour was in 1992 with southern California punk veterans Suicidal Tendencies. Their first album, *Rage Against the Machine*, was released in 1992. The band has sold over fifteen million records worldwide.

In 1993, Rage Against the Machine appeared at Lollapalooza III, on the main stage. But at one show in Philadelphia, they didn't play a single note. Instead, as a silent protest against the censorship of the PMRC (Parents Music Resource Center), they stood naked on stage for fourteen minutes, with duct tape across their mouths and P–M–R–C written on the chests of each of the four band members.

Rage has played numerous concerts in support of a wide array of political causes, including benefits for the England-based Anti-Nazi League, Rock for Choice, for imprisoned Native American Leonard Peltier, and for the Zapatistas. They have donated their earnings to Fairness and Accuracy in Reporting (FAIR), the Zapatista National Liberation Army in Chiapas, Mexico, Women Alive, and organizations supporting Mumia Abu-Jamal.

In 2000, Zack de la Rocha left the band and the remaining three members of Rage Against the Machine formed Audioslave with former Soundgarden singer Chris Cornell. Their self-titled debut was released in 2002. They are currently working on their second album. Morello also records solo guitar and vocals as The Nightwatchman. He continues to donate his time and energy to political causes. His song "No One Left" is featured on the 2004 compilation album *Songs and Artists That Inspired Fahrenheit 9/11* that honors the documentary film by Michael Moore.

About his folk-rock project Morello has said: "The Nightwatchman is my political folk alter ego. I've been writing these songs and playing them at open mic nights with friends for some time." Morello is carrying forward his radical political sensibilities with Nightwatchman lyrics that address the current war in Iraq, the murder of Black Panther activists, and the power of people to bring about revolutionary social change. He also has started a nonprofit organization, Axis of Justice, with Serj Tankian of the band System of a Down. Axis' goal is to "bring together musicians, fans of music, and grassroots political organizations to fight for social justice."

▼ ▼ ▼ ▼ ▼

**John Malkin:** Rage Against the Machine was well-known for its efforts to protest injustice and support positive social change. You have participated in many benefit concerts and rallies and were arrested for civil disobedience during direct actions against sweatshop labor. How important is nonviolence to you as a strategy for cultivating peace and justice?

**Tom Morello:** The history of nonviolent protest is one of many successes. I am not personally wedded to exclusively nonviolent protest. But I think that it can be very effective and it is certainly a preferable way of achieving positive change. If you look at the history of progressive change in the United States, an important lesson I've learned is that we are all historical agents. That history is not something that is made up of names and dates and generals moving pieces around the chessboard. Historically, progressive change comes from average everyday people like you and me. When we stop standing by and start standing up, change happens.

The women's suffrage movement, or the worker's movement for an eight-hour day and an end to child labor, and the Civil Rights movement have all been grassroots movements. Nonviolent strategy has been a crucial part of the history of the United States.

JM: There is a song that Rage Against the Machine recorded, called "Renegades of Funk," that mentions some leaders of social change movements: Chief Sitting Bull, Tom Paine, Dr. Martin Luther King, Jr., and Malcolm X; people, the song says, who have "their own philosophies, who change the course of history." It seems that all of these people also cultivated a spiritual basis for their social action. What do you see as the relationship between inner suffering and the suffering of the world? What is the relationship of spirituality and social change?

TM: "Renegades of Funk" is a cover song that was written by Africa Bambaata. The lyrics are his, but we were very much in agreement with the sentiment expressed in those lyrics. The beginning of a radicalization of a person often stems from an empathy for others and the indignation you feel when you see someone being wronged, whether it is someone in your family, community, or around the globe. Or people around the globe who you see being mal-treated. The impulse to instigate change will often come up. I think that is very true of the activists who are named in that song. You are absolutely right that the one thing that links them is that kind of compassion. I agree that there is a spiritually compassionate core at the center of all great revolutionaries.

JM: Some years ago the Clash sang, in the song "Clampdown,"

Fury has the hour
anger can be power
you know that you can use it.

Your band was named Rage Against the Machine. You were just speaking about the use of empathy and compassion in transforming indignation. What do you think is the use of anger and rage in addressing suffering and bring-ing justice?

TM: I think compassion is a starting point. When you see the harsh realities of a cold capitalist world causing great harm to the environment and to persons along the way, you should be angry! It is at that point that you can either choose to escape by sitting in front of video games or computer screens or television, or you can choose to engage the world and try to funnel that anger into doing the right thing. That is what my heroes have always done. Whether in music, activism, politics, I am most inspired by those who channel their anger into fighting for justice.

JM: On March 21, 2003, the United States government began bombing Iraq again in a full-out war on that country. That evening I saw you perform in San Francisco with Audioslave. There was a sign on stage that read, "How many Iraqis per gallon?" What are your feelings and thoughts now about the U.S. government's attacks and current occupation in Iraq? What is your view of the global justice movement now?

TM: First of all, I think that it should be pointed out that what the antiwar protesters were saying those weeks before the war has been born out entirely. We predicted that an invasion of Iraq would lead to *more* terrorism around the globe and that has happened. We predicted that there were no weapons of mass destruction, that it was a deceit on the part of the Bush administration, and that has proved to be true. There were no tethers between al Qaeda and Saddam Hussein's regime. And all of the justifications for going to war proved to be deceitful.

I think the question then has to be, what were the real reasons for this war? I believe that all you have to do is look at the price of oil and the contracts that have been given out after that.

I have just come off of the Tell Us the Truth Tour with Billy Bragg, Steve Earl, Lester Chamber, Boots Riley, Mike Mills from REM, and Jill Sobule. We toured the country, talking about two issues: media consolidation and corporate globalization. I think that both of those issues are very much tied to our invasion and occupation of Iraq. Media consolidation is one of the reasons why the very complicated issues that everybody needed to process in the wake of 9/11 were simplified into a deceitful, patriotic fog to get this administration's geopolitical agenda across.

Corporate globalization is really at the heart of the matter. Working families here and throughout the world are suffering very much from the multi-nationals' grip on the media and on the levers that control everyday life. But corporate globalization has also brought into effect the movement that will be its undoing. From the WTO riots in Seattle to the enormous protests that we just saw and participated in against the FTAA in Miami, to protests around the globe. People across the globe are uniting against the injustices that corporate globalization is perpetrating.

JM: I hear some people talking about the United States government as being a government that is on the verge of collapse and is losing power and credibility. What do you think about that?

TM: I am not sure. I think that it is wrong to look at the United States government as separate from the corporate entities that bolster it. These organizations, such as the IMF, the WTO, the World Bank—that have no accountability and are not elected—have much control over our air and water and politics and working conditions. We do not vote for them, we do not have anything to do with the decisions that are made, yet they affect so many people's lives. I am not certain that looking at the United States government as separate from those entities is a very helpful model because the decisions that are made on our behalf, on the behalf of Canadians, Mexicans, Guatemalans, and Iraqis, are being made in other places, where they are not accountable.

JM: On March 13, 2001, you met with Mumia Abu-Jamal. You later wrote that, "The most striking thing about the whole experience was how vital, alive, intelligent, humorous, and free Mumia Abu-Jamal seems after having spent twenty-three hours a day for nearly twenty years in a cell smaller then the average bathroom." Tell me more about this visit and your impression of how it is that Mumia has attained freedom within prison.

TM: It was really a pretty amazing day. Rage Against the Machine was a longtime supporter of getting a new trial for Mumia Abu-Jamal. We were playing a show in Pennsylvania and so I paid a visit to the prison there. I was struck by Mumia's vitality. He seemed so much more connected to the world, so much more alive and vital than many people I meet outside of prison. He is constantly writing articles and doing radio interviews and engaging in the world and still fighting for the kind of progressive change that he was doing when he was free and walking among us. It was really a lesson in how one shouldn't waste a minute. Because when someone has the deck stacked against them in the way that he does and he is able to work through that and make such positive contributions, it is very inspirational.

JM: On the cover of Rage Against the Machine's first album is a very dramatic photo of a Buddhist monk named Thich Quang Duc immolating himself in Saigon, Vietnam in 1963. What is the significance of that photo for you and the band?

TM: We thought that image signified an absolutely uncompromising adherence to principle. That is the same kind of uncompromising adherence to principle that we were going for in our band and in our music. So, it seemed like an appropriate symbol to put on the cover.

JM: Where does your impulse to create music come from and how have you been able to incorporate music into your political activism?

TM: First of all, I started playing guitar because of punk rock music. Prior to that I had been a fan of big heavy metal bands. Being a musician seemed very unattainable. I thought you had to have a limo and a castle on a Scottish loch, and $10,000 guitars and whatnot, and a great deal of technical ability in order to make the music I enjoyed hearing. When I got the Sex Pistols' record, that whole idea changed. It was music that was as powerful as anything that I had heard, yet it was attainable. So, I started playing guitar.

I actually joined a band within forty-eight hours of hearing the Sex Pistols' album, without being able to play a single chord on a guitar. Prior to that, I used to draw, write, do art. But as soon as I started playing guitar...I don't know. Sometimes you choose a thing and sometimes it chooses you! That was very much the case with guitar playing for me. It just became an obsessive disorder almost. I would practice up to eight hours a day with the instrument. And it was something I didn't really over-intellectualize. It just came naturally and it felt right and it felt like home. So, I devoted a great deal of time to it.

My twin passions were political activism and rock 'n' roll and they didn't really come together until I was in Rage Against the Machine. Prior to being in Rage Against the Machine, I worked for U.S. Senator Alan Cranston as his scheduling secretary. Alan Cranston, God rest his soul, was a very progressive member of the Senate. But my views were considerably to the left of the offices. But at the time I was playing in another band, Lock Up, that had put out one record on Geffen Records. It was a much more commercial endeavor. And every kind of music industry shafting that can happen, happened to that band. When we were finally dropped from our label, I vowed that I would never again play another note of music that I didn't believe in from my heart. And the next batch of music that I was a part of writing was the first Rage Against the Machine record. That was really a synthesis of our political ideals and the music that we felt the most passionate about making.

In 1991 when it was released, it stood in stark contrast to everything else. There wasn't anything else remotely like it. It was a multiethnic band that combined rock and metal and hip hop with revolutionary neo-Marxist politics. That wasn't exactly a recipe for getting on commercial radio at the time. But, we just believed in it. I think it was that belief and commitment that helped translate our music to a broader audience and really helped bring the politics and the music together in a way that was very natural and was compelling for us, as members of the band. And somehow we found our audience and it was compelling for them too.

# Tom Morello Selected Discography

**With Rage Against the Machine:**
*Rage Against the Machine* – 1992 (Epic)
*Evil Empire* – 1996 (Epic)
*The Battle of Los Angeles* – 1999 (Epic)
*Renegades* – 2000 (Epic)
*Live at the Grand Olympic Auditorium* – 2003 (Epic)

**With Audioslave:**
*Audioslave* – 2002 (Epic)
*Maximum Audioslave* – 2003 (Chrome Dreams)

**As The Nightwatchman:**
*Axis of Justice: Concert Series Volume 1* Compilation Album – 2004
  (Serjical Strike/Columbia)
*Songs and Artists That Inspired Fahrenheit 9/11* Compilation Album – 2004
  (Epic)
*For the Lady* Compilation Album– 2004 (Rhino Records)

# THINKING CLEARLY
# AND BEING FREE

AN INTERVIEW WITH JOHN TRUDELL

We weren't lost
and we didn't need any book
Then the great spirit
met the great lie
Indians are Jesus
Hanging from the cross.
—from "Hanging from the Cross" by John Trudell

WHEN JOHN TRUDELL'S album *Graffiti Man* came out in 1986, Bob
Dylan called it "the best album of 1986." Bonnie Raitt has described Trudell
as "the most charismatic speaker I've ever heard." Kris Kristofferson described
him as "a reality check. Justice is a fire that burns inside him. It makes him
dangerous." And the FBI has called Trudell "an intelligent individual and eloquent speaker."

The FBI quote was discovered among the 17,000 page file that the federal
law enforcement agency had gathered on Trudell, mostly during the 1970s.
The file was obtained through the Freedom of Information Act. Trudell had
been part of the American Indian Movement, one of the organizations that
the U.S. government sought to disrupt, discredit, and destroy through the
FBI's Counter Intelligence Program (COINTELPRO).

John Trudell was born on February 15, 1946 in Omaha, Nebraska, the son
of a Santee Sioux father and a Mexican mother. He was raised around the
Santee reservation near Omaha. He is a veteran of the U.S. war in Vietnam.
After getting out of the military in 1967 he attended college for some time

before moving on to participate in the social change movements that were developing at the time.

In 1969, Trudell was part of a group called Indians of All Tribes that occupied Alcatraz Island in the San Francisco Bay. The group reclaimed the island under the authority of an 1868 federal treaty that allowed Native Americans use of federal territory that the U.S. government was not actively using. Alcatraz had been a federal prison until 1963, when it was closed down. On June 11, 1971, nineteen months after Trudell and others occupied the island, federal marshals removed the fifteen Indians from Alcatraz by force.

Following the Indians of All Tribes occupation of Alcatraz, Trudell worked with the American Indian Movement (AIM) and served as their national chairman from 1972 until 1979. In 1979, Trudell gave a speech on the steps of the FBI building in Washington, D.C., protesting the agency's persecution of members of AIM. He burned an American flag to emphasize his point. The next day, on February 12, 1979, his mother-in-law, wife, and three children were killed in a house fire on the Shoshone Paiute reservation in Nevada. The fire was never investigated. Trudell had at least twice received warnings from strangers that his family was in danger unless he gave up his political activity. He believes that the fire was deliberately set and was an act of murder.

The tragedy of losing his loved ones motivated Trudell to write poetry and begin performing spoken word and music infused with indigenous wisdom, critical thinking, and an examination of culture and relations in the United States. He used words and music to transform his anger and grief into art.

In 1979 he met Jackson Browne, who led Trudell into the world of music and performance. Browne helped to record Trudell's first tape in 1982, *Tribal Voices*, which was a synthesis of spoken word and traditional Native music.

In 1985, Trudell met Jesse Ed Davis, a Kiowa guitarist who was already a well-known musician. They recorded three albums together, bringing together a sound that defined Trudell's early works. Davis died in 1988. Mark Shark would later become Trudell's guitarist.

Trudell is currently the cultural advisor for the All Tribes Foundation. He has published three books of poetry and has supported the growth of independent media and community radio.

For over three decades, John Trudell's deep and confident voice has spoken out against the global corporate tyranny that is damaging the Earth, separating people, creating economic injustice, and disturbing indigenous peoples worldwide. Trudell sums up his intentions with these words: "My goal is very simple. To communicate the human experience at a level that human beings can recognize and can relate to."

▼ ▼ ▼ ▼ ▼

**John Malkin**: You have said that you don't trust the "corporate democracy" of the United States and that you see social change coming from culture, art, and music rather than politics. How did you transform your political activism into your spoken word and music work?

**John Trudell**: Well, I will see if I can remember all of that territory. My attitude about democracy isn't limited to corporate democracy, although that seems to be what we are dominated by at this time. I question the concept of political democracy itself. Historically speaking, all democratic societies have had class systems. All democratic societies were sexist. At some point or another, slavery was a part of their trip. And all democratic societies were never really based on majority rule. Actually, the concept of political democracy basically comes down to, as Noam Chomsky says, the idea of the right of the entitled to rule.

American democracy is allegedly about majority rule, but when the founders created the Constitution, they also decided that if you were a native person, you were the enemy. Even though we were the majority! And if you were a woman, you were considered mentally incompetent. It was men's business and you had no say. If you were black, you were property. If you were a white male who did not own land, you had no taxable value, so you had no say. None of these parties got to vote in this "majority rule" democracy. The only people who got to vote were that small group of white, male landowners. The founders created a system for those who considered themselves entitled so that they would rule. That is the way that it started out and it seems to me that that's the way it is still practiced, for the most part, today.

I think we are now at a high-tech age where American democracy is more like guerrilla theater and the audience gets to participate. They hype up these big elections every year and billions of dollars get spent and people get to participate and get to *believe* that they mean something in this process. And at the same time, people participating in the process are being lied to by the political system. The politicians in this gradual erosion are more and more in the corporate pocket. That industrial ruling class seem to be the only ones that this democracy works for.

JM: What do you think is the way out of this and what role do music and art play in transformation?

JT: I don't know about the way out. Right now the whole system does not seem to be designed in any type of way to live in harmony with the Earth. It seems to me that every human being is the descendant of a tribe. Every human being. And I think that the way of the tribe is the way that human beings are meant to live with the Earth. The way of the tribe is based around the philosophy that we are physical entities in a spiritual reality. And that all things have a spiritual value. Our purpose as human beings is to live in balance with the living entity that is Earth and to use the time that we are here on Earth to take care of the Earth so that the next generation and the next generation can continue their responsibility to also keep a balance with the Earth.

Before the industrial beast rose up with its many disguises, we lived to keep a balance with the Earth. And this is when we had the most power ever as human beings. I think that living with the Earth and maintaining a balance is the way that we are supposed to live. That is the only way that we will get to continue in the evolutionary reality of the human being. If we get so far out of balance with the Earth, then at some point, in some kind of a way, we will extinguish ourselves.

When you live with the Earth, you don't own it, you are a part of it. You are a part of the sky and the universe. You live to live in balance. I think that we can relearn to live this way, even with technology and industry. Because it is based on an understanding that life has a spiritual value and that spiritual value emanates from the Earth. You know, you break it down for who we are, our DNA, our bone, flesh and blood: we are made up of the metals, minerals, and liquids of the Earth. We are shapes of the Earth. We are a part of this Earth. The Earth truly and literally is our mother.

We, as human beings, need to take the responsibility of using our intelligence as clearly and coherently as we can. We need to think. We live in a society now where there is actually very little thinking going on. Ninety percent of the time we are emotionally reacting to our beliefs and our rages and our angers. We don't really participate in our communities with clear and coherent thinking. And it manifests in our individual lives and it manifests through the collective society itself.

JM: What has helped you in being able to "use your intelligence intelligently," as you have said, and not be simply reactive?

JT: I am going to clarify that phrase, "using my intelligence clearly and coherently." I didn't wake up one day and decide to be as clear and coherent as I possibly could. But somewhere in the course of living my life, I came to understand that knowing isn't enough. When I was younger, I wanted to know all the answers. But, I have to *understand* what I know! Somewhere in the course of my life, I am coming to understand that it is important to reach an understanding with this reality that we are in. Like anyone, I can be coherent and I can be clear. I can also be unclear and incoherent. I work at trying to understand using coherence and clarity especially when it is necessary. We have to think beyond our beliefs. Believing is just another way of saying, "I don't know." It sedates the mind. So, if we don't know, then we should think. Thinking stimulates the mind. Our mind's purpose is to think and to create.

We truly do have to be careful of simply reacting emotionally to our beliefs and fears and rages. It isn't just the right wing doing it, the left is doing it, too. And the in-betweens are doing it. Nobody is thinking clearly. It is difficult to just blame, say, the industrial right wing. Because if the Right is playing the music and we continue to dance to it, then we have to think about our complicity in this. What is our role? It is not about judging others or ourselves. It is just about thinking and getting a clear understanding of what is going on.

We all have the ability to think clearly. It evolves with our experiences and certain choices and decisions that we make. We get old so that we can understand more. But we live in a society where people are afraid to get old.

JM: You have spoken of the importance of trusting yourself and liking yourself. In another interview, you said, "There is no collective solution without an individual solution." Tell me more about that.

JT: Again, it's about how we perceive reality, because as human beings how we manifest the reality of our powers is through our perception of reality. We have to, individually, recognize ourselves and then accept ourselves. It is important that we don't judge ourselves, but rather recognize who we are. How are we going to create peace and balance if we can't do it inside ourselves? It is not possible.

We haven't done anything wrong. We have all made mistakes in our lives. Every one of us. But we live in an environment where we're programmed from birth to judge ourselves for the mistakes we make. We always judge ourselves negatively. We're not taught to recognize the reality of who we are. Life is a continuing experience. We were given intelligence and the ability to have understanding so that we would learn from our experiences. From our unhealthy experiences, we can learn balance. But we were never supposed to judge our experiences, they are just meant to help us to recognize the reality of who we are. Once we accept that and put ourselves into a balance, then we can start to create a larger balance in the world.

In our industrial society, our perception of power is that it is in external things. It is in money, guns, votes, clothes, whatever. But for us as natural, spiritual entities, as human beings, our power is a part of who we are. It is not something external. It is a part of our consciousness and our intelligence. Our power is our essence.

If individually we start to use this power, very clearly and coherently, then it will spread. More and more people will see it and be affected by it and start to transform themselves. This is the only way we're going to bring any real solutions to this planet in this lifetime.

JM: Some political activists, recognizing that organized religions have been used to justify war, genocide, and destruction, have discarded religion. Some of them have discarded spirituality as well. I think people sometimes feel like they need to choose between social change and spiritual growth. I wonder what you think about that?

JT: I think that they are too busy dividing stuff up. Number one, I think that there is a difference between spirituality and religion. I think that religion has absolutely nothing to do with spirituality. It never did. All right? If you really want to be logical about it and understand the mechanisms of history, religion is a spirit hunter. Religion has been one of the biggest tools used to break the spirit of people who didn't have religion. It's been used to consume the spirit of people who were believed to be without religion, by Judeo-Christian definitions.

If you look at the amount of destruction that has been wreaked on this planet with religious motive and religious justification, it has been very brutal and very, very violent. So much life—millions of people, but also so many different kinds of plant and animal life—has been destroyed in the name of religion. Religion is like a machine that was created by man to control other human beings. Spirit is what we are born with as human beings. Spirit is what we have. We're born with it. And we will have it, in some shape or form, until we leave this reality. Our spirit is part of the essence of who we are.

For people who go looking for their spirituality, I think the best way to look is to recognize. The best way to show respect for our community, or for the nation, or the self or the next generation, is to be real to ourselves. That is a part of that spiritual search. Who am I? I am a spirit. We need to ask ourselves, What am I capable of? What have I done? Do I accept the whole of who I am? Do I accept even the parts of my behavior I don't like? Do I accept that as being a part of the whole of who I am or do I wander off into denial and blame? It is about making an understanding *of* self *with* the self. And that cannot help but have the effect of being a positive force for whatever it is that we would call the social change or the good that we want to do in the world.

JM: In 1986, Bob Dylan said that your album *AKA Graffiti Man* was the best album of the year.

JT: He was right!

JM: You were called "extremely eloquent" by the Federal Bureau of Investigation. Apparently you got hold of 17,000 pages of FBI documents from their investigation of you. What was your experience with the FBI during that time? I know that you were involved in a lot of activism with the American Indian Movement (AIM) during that time and you helped to occupy Alcatraz Island and you gave speeches all over the country. Tell me about that time period and how that led to you channeling your focus and energy and political activism into spoken word and music.

JT: Between 1969 and 1979 was the hardcore activist time. That was my whole center. I started in 1969 with Alcatraz and then went to AIM and was involved in most of the AIM things during the seventies. We had our different little run-ins with different law enforcement agencies, from the Washington, D.C. Metro police to small vigilante groups in Pawnee, Oklahoma. But these were obvious confrontations, high and intense and out in the open.

I knew that the FBI was around and I had encountered them and I had figured that they had infiltrated AIM and that they were around in ways that weren't obvious. But I was shocked! When we went to the Freedom of Information files in 1980, the year after my family was killed, and I found that I had 17,000 pages that basically covered a ten year time frame...I am still surprised. I am truly surprised. Because I did nothing to warrant that. I was never really a political threat or an economic threat. Definitely not a military threat. I wasn't a religious threat. It made me wonder, What is the reason for their fanaticism around this? But then it came back to me that sometimes I can be really coherent and that is what later started to make me think about that. The fact of all of those pages is overwhelming to me! I know what I did and didn't do and there is no way that there is any reasonable justification for that extreme level of surveillance.

But it says something, that little blurb from the FBI, that I can be "extremely eloquent." That is when I started to understand. See, they don't care what we *do*. They just don't want us to think clearly and be coherent. They fear somebody being coherent and clear and communicating that to another person. That is the power they fear coming out of the people. They don't worry whether you vote or not. They *want* you to vote because you are always going to lose in this system. You are never going to win. But if you think clearly and coherently for yourself, then you become a threat to them. They know that this is all a big mind game.

In a way, that is what started to change my understanding, to give me a different understanding. We did the confrontation stuff. We occupied the BIA and took over Wounded Knee and occupied Alcatraz and probably another hundred or so little occupations and all of that stuff. We went through the court systems and did all of that. I had that whole experience. That's how I got all of these pages. But then after my family was killed, and I was in this limbo madness, and that Freedom of Information came back with the thousands of pages, somewhere in that time frame I started to get this understanding that the only thing that is a true threat to them is clear, independent, coherent thinking. Somebody wants to have armed rebellion? Well, that's profitable to them. They make a lot of money out of that.

It was during that period of time that I started to write. I didn't make a conscious decision. I didn't just decide, "Well, I am going to start writing poetry." I started writing poetry and after I had started to write for awhile and realize that I was writing, *then* I made a conscious decision that I would follow the spoken word, the poetry. I would follow the lines to where it took me. And it led to working with music.

By the time I started writing and working with the music, it was clear in my mind that the political stuff, you deal with it the way that you have to, but there is not going to be any real change coming there because that is all reactive. Everybody is reacting to their emotions about the "bad guys" or what they like and don't like, but it doesn't necessarily mean that people are clearly thinking things out. By identifying ourselves so politically, we were limiting our view. For AIM and Native people, this definitely isn't our political system. And it's not the black people's political system. And if you want to be realistic about it, it's not the political system of the whites either. It's the political system of that industrial ruling class.

At that point I came to understand that only through culture and art, for us as Native people, only through our culture and our art can we express the realities of who we are. Because if we only believe the political aspect of it, we can never express our truths through that because we are too emotionally worked up. The political system is designed so that you can't really express your truths. You can express your emotional reactions, but you can't really express your truths.

JM: You have said, "We should always tell ourself the truth." What do you think is the relationship between truth and freedom?

JT: The truth? The truth is that freedom is a lie. This is what I mean about thinking about things, all right? I think that the big obsession and chase for freedom is just a heroin trip for our consciousness. Freedom has absolutely nothing to do with it. Life is about responsibility. And if we as individual human beings would use our intelligence, the gift our creator gave us as human beings to participate and maintain a balance in this reality, then we will be taking responsibility. Once we take responsibility, we will enter into the reality of being free.

In the late 1960s, with the political movements and Native communities and all of the other social movements going on—antiwar, women's rights—every one of us was wanting our freedom. But when I think back on it, maybe our whole mindset should have been, "We're going to take responsibility. We are going to use our intelligence and take responsibility." Everybody has been chasing freedom, but nobody wants responsibility. The net result is the situation that we are in.

I don't trust the concept of freedom. I understand the concept of being free. I understand that. That makes perfect sense to me. *Being free.* But freedom is just a habitual, lazy abstraction. What does it mean? What does freedom mean? If I were to say to the world, "I believe in freedom," I would be lying. Would that mean that I also believe that the racist has the freedom to be racist? That the class monger has the freedom to be a class monger? That people who send young people off to die in wars for profit have the freedom to do that? If I decide that I believe in freedom, if it is real, then I have to accept their freedom to do that. And I think that all of those freedoms are irresponsible.

We need to make some distinctions about how we participate in this reality. Life is about responsibility. Why are we so afraid to explore that and understand that? That is how this beast has eluded us all of these years. People have been rebelling against responsibility for centuries. Somehow our perception of reality has become so distorted that we don't participate clearly. Freedom is an abstraction. Responsibility is not. And if we want to *be free*, then we have to understand that difference.

There are levels of being free. Number one, the first place of being free is being free within our own consciousness. To accept, understand, and know who we are. Every word has its own meaning because every word makes its own individual sound. So when we say a word, we're putting sound out into a vibratory reality, which has its effect. It is like throwing a stone in a pond. So, when we use a word like "freedom", it makes its own sound, it has its own meaning. Or if we use two words and say, "being free" or "be free," it has its own sound and its own meaning. And I trust the sounds of "being free" more then I trust the sound of "freedom." Because freedom automatically turns its back on responsibility.

Whatever the predator energy is, whether it is government or corporations or whatever it is, it is easy for us to point at it because it is there and it is so obvious. But if we're ever going to challenge it, if we're ever going to get past it, we have to look at ourselves and see how we dance to their music. Maybe we're just dancing to the wrong songs. Our responsibility is to use our intelligence to recognize things, not to judge them. Because if we recognize, we see it clearly and it will influence the next decisions that we make. Many people don't want to hear this.

JM: Why not?

JT: Because people are afraid of the idea of responsibility. This whole concept of saying to people, "Look, we really need to think clearly," can be very confusing. When that situation exists, I wonder, "Well, why don't we think better of ourselves?" To me it is about low self-esteem.

JM: There seems to be an epidemic of that in the United States.

JT: That is because it is programmed in us since birth. In this society, let's just say in this country, it goes on other places too, but in this particular country from birth, we're programmed to view ourselves negatively. By the time that we become adults, we may hide it behind a mask of pride or other behaviors, but everybody has to dance with their demons. It is almost as if we have been programmed not to like ourselves. Definitely we have been programmed not to recognize ourselves. And if we can't recognize ourselves, then obviously we won't really trust or like ourselves.

There is nothing wrong with us. This is how this thing is passed through the generations. If you get that first generation programmed that class systems are okay, then it is an easy matter to program the next generation. Once you get that first generation programmed with, "sexism is okay," then it's a lot easier to perpetuate the program into the following generations. Once you program that first generation, that spiritual value is removed from the Earth and the Earth isn't really about what life is all about, it is easier to program that into the next generation. It is all programming.

People who do relate to a creator—whether it is through religion, God, or spirit—out of respect for that creator, they should always be real to themselves about what their behaviors and thoughts are. They should not hide behind denial or rationalization. We should always be real to ourselves because otherwise we are not respecting the creator. So, we weaken the good we want to accomplish if we're not showing respect.

JM: How do you think conditions have changed for Native Americans since the 1970s and how aware do you think other Americans are of the history and presence of Native Americans?

JT: First of all, I think that Native people have opened up on the concept of sovereignty a little bit, so you have these gaming governments and the tribes are making a few more decisions on their own and things like that. But in reality, we, the Native people of this country, are still colonized by the American government through organizations and the Bureau of Indian Affairs, the Department of Justice, and the Department of Interior. In the end, the final decisions are still made at those levels.

In some reservations, the poverty is more extreme, or just as extreme as it was thirty years ago. There are places like Pine Ridge where you still have eighty percent unemployment. It's more extreme in the sense that the laws are harsher now and part of the government solution now is to criminalize people rather then to help them to solve the social issues that are causing these problems. There are more young natives getting access to an education, but in the long run I don't know how healthy that is if it is just more brainwashing. Young people may retain their pride, but if they're not given knowledge that can help them really go back and help change the social conditions of the community, then I have questions about that kind of education.

I think that your average American doesn't have a clue what is happening to Native people, I don't mean this as an insult or any sign of disrespect. It's just they don't have a clue what is happening to themselves. They just know that they are losing their jobs. They know they can't pay the rent and can't afford health insurance. They've got so many troubles themselves and they can't recognize the cause of their problems. They are blaming a political party rather than an economically created political system. So, I don't expect them to have any real understanding of what is happening to Native Americans because they can't even see what is happening to them! I think most Americans are desperate to believe in promises and blame.

JM: One more question. The United States government has led a lot of wars over the years and usually they in fact do say that it is to bring freedom and democracy to the world.

JT: That's when you know you're in trouble, man! You know you're in it, now.

JM: Yeah, it usually arrives in the form of bullets and bombs. So, the United States has recently been warring on Iraq. You were a soldier in the Vietnam war and I wonder what your view is on the current so-called War on Terrorism, the war in Iraq, and what you might say to young people who might be considering joining the military or who may, in the not too distant future, be facing a reinstated draft in this country?

JT: The war in Iraq is just plain wrong. And the war in Iraq has everything to do with oil. So did the war in Afghanistan. Central Asia has the largest amount of oil resources that exist in the world. To get those goods out of there, they have to go through Afghanistan. Whoever controls those resources, they get to dominate the world for the next hundred years.

The war in Iraq is disguised in these religious overtones and these crusade overtones, the way [war and conquest] were disguised a thousand years ago. It is really about money. It is about blood for profit. It is about blood for world domination. You know, freedom and democracy, all of that stuff…I place it in the context of native people. Before we heard the word freedom or democracy, we were free and we were living in a balance. So, it is obvious to me by this time that what is going on in Iraq is really about world domination and economics.

Because of the United States' policies and treatment of others in the world, we have this terrorist war. I think that war should be fought if one is attacked. But to wage a real war against terrorism, you would have to fight the Enrons and the corporate corruption and the government corruption that is going on with the creation of these Super Patriot Acts and all of the corruption that is going on at the ruling class level. All that is terrorism. When you manipulate the economics the way that they have been manipulated, it creates—we'll use Enron as the example—all of these workers and all of these citizens who now suffer economically and as a result of suffering, they now fear. They wonder, "How am I going to pay my rent? How am I going to afford to send my kid to school? How am I going to afford medical coverage?" Is that not the result of terror? Is that not the objective of terrorism, to create fear? To destabilize a society and create fear? I think that we need to define the entirety of what terrorism is if we're going to talk about war on it.

The question I would ask any young person who was thinking about joining the army is, "Why?" I would ask them to think this thing out. Because joining the army is not about saving America. It's about industrial ruling class greed. I would like to think that people at any age, but especially the young, would not want to be used in that kind of a way. That they would have a better grasp of life. It's not in their best interests.

You brought up this thing about the draft. I am sure that the draft is going to come back. It is obvious that we can't out-fight them. Since the Romans, and probably longer than that, the oppressed never did out-fight the oppressor without becoming the new oppressor themselves. But I think that we can out-think them. That is the value of using our intelligence. We are still in a position where we can exercise and use the real power that we represent. The power of the people. Not power *to* the people, the power *of* the people. The power of the people is in clear, coherent, individual, collective thought.

# John Trudell Selected Discography

*Tribal Voice* – 1983 (Peace Company Productions)

*AKA Graffiti Man* – 1986/1992 (Peace Company Productions/
  Rykodisc Records)

*...But This Isn't El Salvador* – 1987 (Tribal Voice)

*Heart Jump Bouquet* – 1987 (Peace Company Productions)

*Fables and Other Realities* – 1991 (Peace Company Productions)

*Child's Voice: Children of the Earth* – 1992 (Peace Company Productions)

*Johnny Damas & Me* – 1994 (Rykodisc Records)

*Blue Indians* – 1999 (Dangerous Discs on Inside Recordings)

*Descendant Now Ancestor* – 2001 (ASITIS Productions)

*Bone Days* – 2001 (ASITIS Productions)

# BE THE CHANGE YOU WANT TO SEE

## An Interview with Rickie Lee Jones

Revolution
Now it's finally going to come
Everywhere that you're not looking
Revolution
And we'll take the country back
Everywhere that you're not looking.
—from "Ugly Man" by Rickie Lee Jones

RICKIE LEE JONES has long offered the world soulful music and heartfelt
words that resonate with the universal needs for intimacy, love, and connection. She is best known for revealing the tender side of human relationships,
shedding light on the sorrow that comes with losing love. Jones has experi-
mented with a variety of musical directions during her career, but she hadn't
been known for her political analysis or calls for social action, until her political awakening during the Clinton presidential administration years.

On her 2003 release *Evening of My Best Day*, the catchy jazz-infused
melodies that Jones has long been identified with now serve as foundations
for commenting on the policies of the president of the United States ("He's
an ugly man, just like his father"), the stealing of the 2000 presidential elections ("Little mysteries, down in Florida"), and encouraging people to take
action to preserve civil liberties being threatened by laws like the Patriot Act
("Tell somebody, what's happening in the USA, rise up!").

Rickie Lee Jones was born on November 8, 1954 in Chicago, Illinois, into
a family she has described as "lower-middle-class-hillbilly-hipster." By the
time she graduated from high school, her family had lived in California, Arizona, and Washington. The family of three daughters and one son was often

scraping by. Jones' mother, Bettye, had grown up as an orphan and worked as a waitress and later as a nurse. A thread of showbusiness runs through her family: her father, Richard, was a performer who traveled the country as a hobo and Jones' grandfather, Peg Leg, had been a one-legged vaudeville dancer. It was her father who first taught Rickie Lee how to sing and in her early concerts, Jones would perform, "The Moon Is Made of Gold," a lullaby that her father had written for her.

At fourteen, after her parents had separated, she was living with her father in Arizona, and she ran away, hitchhiking across three states. After high school, Rickie Lee Jones began singing and writing lyrics more and more.

In 1973, when she was eighteen, Jones moved to Venice, California, and a year later was waiting tables and occasionally playing music at coffee houses and bars in Los Angeles. Her music caught the attention of Little Feat founder Lowell George, who recorded Jones' song, "Easy Money" on his solo album *Thanks, I'll Eat It Here*. In 1976 she met Sal Bernardi and they collaborated for years to come. During this period, Jones started to write more original songs and perform them with Alfred Johnson at the Ala Carte Club in Hollywood.

In 1979, Warner released her first album, *Rickie Lee Jones*. The album was nominated for five Grammy Awards that year including Best Record, and won the Grammy for Best New Artist. Not only did her album make an immediate impact, but her original style of dressing—with beret, dress, and heels—would influence the counterculture in the United States.

Rickie Lee Jones' website is called Furniture for the People. Its is an "online community featuring a Free Press, a message board, and an opportunity to help others." The site includes recommended political reading, including the 1992 Nobel Peace Prize speech of Rigoberta Menchu, an article about Catholic Worker founder Dorothy Day, and an analysis of the 2003 Patriot Act II. There are also links to social change organizations. During the 2004 U.S. presidential campaigns, visitors to the website were invited to submit essays on, "Why I support my candidate for president."

Jones has always focused on art and expression, and not on marketing. True to self, not wanting to go with corporate record companies, she has turned down requests for use of her music in television commercials, including a bank that offered her "a lot of money," according to her online journal. She has held a strong ethical stand against commodifying and commercializing her music, though her style has been copied, and much to her dismay, an unauthorized sampling of her voice found its way into a car commercial. She wound up having to sell the rights to her songs to raise money for the production of her latest album, *The Evening of My Best Day*.

Rickie Lee Jones is an artist with a remarkable ability to open her most vulnerable side to the audience. On her website, she writes, "Of course it's cool to play, but it's terrifying, every night wondering if you'll perform, in this limited space, according to your and their hopes and expectations, wondering with each step if it will take you where you hope to go."

I met Jones backstage after a show, where she was cherishing the last bites of an ice cream sundae. We sat at one of the round tables in the now dimly lit, empty club and talked about her music, spirituality, and ideas about the prospects for revolutionary change in the United States. Jones is an artist preaching to the not-yet converted, and doing it with the rich vocal style and jazz instrumentation that has made her music so well-loved.

▼ ▼ ▼ ▼ ▼

**John Malkin**: A lot of the songs from your latest CD, *The Evening of My Best Day* are about the Patriot Act and about George W. Bush. Tonight you urged the audience to become active and take a role in the revolution. You seem to bring that message to people directly.

You have said that you never cared about politics in the past, but that changed the year that George W. Bush was selected president. Tell me about your political awakening.

**Ricki Lee Jones**: It started before George Bush. I think my understanding of the political system really happened when Bill Clinton was in office. When the newspapers published the lowdown on his sexual exploits—and I didn't read them—I thought that some notch had turned where our country had been degraded so much.

For many of us who lived through it, the sixties were about the polarization between the "established population" and the younger generation, the hippies, the "long hairs," and the antiwar citizens. The establishment felt violent animosity towards the very idea of being critical of the government or any American social customs. To have long hair, especially as a man, became tantamount to treason.

I say this to remind you how far we have come. Because at the time there was a basic breakdown of the respect that every citizen is due in this country, regardless of their beliefs. The Civil Rights movement was still sinking in. With the racism and the prejudice in our society, there had been a breakdown in our basic goodness as a society that should treat all people fairly.

I think a breakdown is occurring again right now, manufactured by right-wing extremists with little moral fiber. With the publication of Clinton's sexual exploits, we allowed our president to be publicly eviscerated by privately funded persons. We allowed our children to read newspapers describing this very private, albeit disgraceful, behavior. We changed our moral character at that moment and we have been on a slippery slope ever since.

The way this country and its elections are being orchestrated by corrupt officials, and the obvious exhaustion of our citizens, is what has brought me to fight for this country I grew up in. I want to keep our naive and powerful image of this country as a democracy intact. That is what I am fighting for. I am not a socialist or a communist. I am not interested in ideology. I am just fighting for the ideals of the past two hundred years.

JM: What are your main concerns about the Patriot Act?

RLJ: My main concern is that it will be used to stop all voices of dissent. In the last three years that Bush has been in office, it seems people are just afraid to criticize him. I have never seen fear to that extent in my life. If the government could create that much of a culture of fear without the Patriot Act, it's scary to imagine what they can do now that they have the Patriot Act to legally back them up. What frightens me most is that the act will be used to suppress our own people in any manner that the government sees fit.

JM: You have received some criticism for this political material on your new CD. There was an article in the *L.A. Times* magazine that said that the new album "reveals an unlikely activist persona." Other artists, actors and musicians have been criticized for speaking out against the Bush regime and against the war in Iraq. Did it feel difficult or dangerous for you to make that CD?

RLJ: It wasn't difficult at all, because the words were just what flowed naturally from me as a writer. As a mother, as a human being living in America, as an American, there was no way I could *not* say something. Because nobody was saying anything. I had to say something. So, I could not have *not* spoken up.

JM: Millions of people were involved in nonviolent protests against this most recent U.S. war on Iraq, yet the bombing happened anyway. I wonder what your view is of the current global justice and antiwar movements.

RLJ: George W. Bush tends to do whatever he wants to do, regardless of what the people indicate that they want. You can see that in policies ranging from drilling for oil to the cutting back of funds for Medicare. People have made clear that they didn't want that, but he did it anyway. His first order of business, as a president declaring war, was to assign who would get the contracts to rebuild. He didn't even try to disguise that this war was just to create business and money for certain people.

He is using the grief and fear of Americans after 9/11 to fuel his greed. But shame on the Americans for letting him do so! I think they know what he is doing and now they don't want to look.

JM: What is your view on nonviolence as a strategy for social change?

RLJ: I think that the nonviolent protests against the Iraq war were really powerful. The question has to be, what can nonviolent protest accomplish? One of the things it can do right now is bring the message to people that peace lovers are still here. We are still protesting, we people who will not be defeated, we people who are fighting this fascist footnote in our democracy.

Men especially are so inclined to want to commit acts of violence and want to start wars. They are! My hope for peace really is that women participate in government and insist that the feminine aspect be delivered. I think that women can provide the balance that our political system needs. I hope that they step up.

As a country we are so violent. The American people don't know it because they have never been anyone else. If they could just see we don't have to be afraid for our children to walk from here to the store. Lots of countries are not. The violence that takes place on every corner every week is an aberration. It does not have to be all we are or all that we do.

Americans could just learn that they won't lose their individuality and their strength and character by becoming more peaceful. All of the things that make us so unique and powerful and wonderful—we won't lose them!

JM: You have said that this latest record is the culmination of a great deal of spiritual energy and of your wanting to have the rest of your life be a good life. What role does spirituality play in your life? What do you think is the relationship between spirituality and social change? By spirituality, I mean a cultivating of compassion and kindness towards self and others and a wisdom about the interconnectedness between things.

RLJ: It just seems obvious that you couldn't do one without the other. To me they are one and the same.

JM: On the *Ghostyhead* album you sing in "Cloud of Unknowing" "I long to enter you with gentleness and compassion, but sorrow is always the open door." Many spiritual traditions acknowledge sorrow and suffering as the possible opening to happiness and joy. I wonder what that line means to you, "sorrow is always the open door"?

RLJ: That is a many-hued question. I sang that song twice tonight because I saw a girl was crying at the front of the stage. I think that sometimes the only way to connect with other people is if you turn with a great wave of your sorrow. It is just some kind of alchemy. If you open up to people, their hearts will respond.

In love, I have found sometimes that empathy and compassion are the only doors. Sometimes this is the only way I can reach my daughter. When we feel bad, we often think others want to fight with us. But when we show compassion to the sorrow of other human beings, then we can say, "You must feel really bad." Then they say, "Ahh," and open up.

The line about opening sorrow's door is very, very spiritual, obviously, but it is also meant to rest very comfortably with the sensuality and sexuality of it as well.

JM: Tell me about the song "Ugly Man." How did that come together?

RLJ: Every time I see George Bush on TV I get so mad. He seems so contemptuous. He gets angry if he is asked a question he doesn't like. So, every time I'd see him on TV, smug and contemptuous, it would make me angry and that was what came out of that melody. I'd been messing around with that line and it just happened. Instantly. I liked it. I hesitated slightly because it was a mean lyric and the melody is so pretty. I didn't know if I wanted that, but that melody wanted that lyric.

My sense is that those old jazz guys would be happy with that song. Whoever they are, wherever they are. I always saw in my mind the Black Panthers coming and standing in back of it when the regal horns blow. There they are, standing all around, empowering me.

JM: A lot of public people don't change their minds publicly. In your career, you have changed your music and lyrics as you have changed. It takes some courage to do that.

RLJ: You know, I learn as I go. In show business, and as consumers also, people like things to stay the same. And if you change, they are uncertain of your new image. For me, maybe it is partly because I am a musician, I have a little more leeway. I might lose a lot of people as I change and my music changes, but when I am done, I will have designed a new genre for somebody else to elaborate in their own lives.

As far as I am concerned, through will and accident, I have created my own way. Also, I don't do well following. If I succeeded as a follower, I would probably do it. Ultimately, I want to be happy, and I am happiest doing it the way that I do it.

JM: That is great that you have found happiness.

RLJ: Well, happiness is relative. If you have joyful moments, then you are happy, I think.

JM: You have refused to sell your music for use in television commercials. Why?

RLJ: Well, the first word that comes to mind is *sacred*. Music is important to people. They have assigned pivotal moments to the lyrics or the melody and then it seems wrong to give it to a car! I just think it is wrong. People need to have these pieces of music that are important to them. But when I was broke and I needed some money, I did sell the rights to my lyrics so that I could have the money to make this latest record.

JM: In the song "Ugly Man," you sing about revolution. You say, "Now it is finally going to come, everywhere that you're not looking." Tell me what you think revolution requires and how you think the idea of revolution has changed in this country since the 1960s.

RLJ: The line says, "It is happening everywhere you're not looking." So revolution is happening in a quiet way. In the back of my mind, though not so far back, I was again thinking of the Black Panthers. None of us wants to be violent. At some point we all have to draw the real line of who we really are. Then, in my heart of hearts, I feel that I could never kill anyone.

The revolution that I advocate is one that is probably not possible because it is to restore or retain an ethic that we have had as Americans. I am not sure if we can do that. It is a revolution that tops Fox News. So, I suppose it is a romantic line.

JM: Do you think that revolution is possible?

RLJ: I only know from reading in books. And those revolutions go on forever. They are bloody, millions die. It seems to me that countries don't get any better after the revolutions. I think that we have to save this country. We can't go kill it and tear it down. But we are a relatively new country.

JM: Linked to your website there is a political information center called Furniture for the People. The website offers articles by and about people like Dorothy Day and Iranian activist and Nobel Peace Prize winner Shirin Ebadi. Tell me about Furniture for the People.

RLJ: It's maintained primarily by my friend Lee Cantalon who is a graphic designer and activist. He is very left-wing and very articulate and able to give the boundless energy that it takes to do this. He teaches me a lot. I wanted to create a political area for people to go. Actually, it was a kind of spiritual response because I was thinking the current government is putting out violence and it is representing us. I wanted to offer the website as a little bit of good in America's name.

That is really what it is for me—to create some good so that spiritually, maybe this one little grain of sand would have mattered. That was my hope for the website. It could really be a networking place, aside from the political, it could have a great impact locally.

JM: In an essay you quote Ursula K. Le Guin from her book *Sixty Odd* where she says: "The only thing that makes life possible is permanent, intolerant uncertainty." Tell me a little more about your journey of following your own vision amidst uncertainty and dealing with uncertainty in not knowing what is going to happen to one's career, one's life, not knowing how long one is going to live. You're taking chances and risks in your career when there was a lot of pressure to not do that.

RLJ: Maybe it is because I am forty-nine. I can't tell if it has to do with my chronological age or just a series of events that happened to people I love—but I could see that I would die. I was imagining that I died and was still here, and I turned and looked at my life and all the things that I could have done, but hesitated because of fear, and I decided that there is nothing to be afraid of. The only thing to be afraid of is that you are going to die and you are going to die anyway, so why be afraid? If you live your life like you don't want to die, then you've lived your whole life afraid. And in this picture I saw, all of us human beings were always safe. We were always safe. We were never *not* safe. We were safe when we died, we were safe for the whole journey. I don't know how I saw that, but it is like I have already died and now I am turning back and living my life not so afraid. I mean, my internal machine is worn, so I have internal emotional struggles, but for the most part, in the outside life, I am not afraid. I feel very, very glad to be alive.

I look at people with a lot of hope and compassion. I talk to them and am interested in healing them. I see my life as planting a lot of little flowers that will be here after I go.

JM: You were just talking about having hope and you sing on *The Evening of My Best Day*, "Look ahead, the sky is almost blue." Where does your hope come from?

RLJ: I can tell you that my hope is generated when I pray. When I don't pray, when I forget to sit and say "thank you," I become depleted. And when I do pray, I feel like I leave behind the big ball of ego. When I pray, things just go through me and they don't get stuck in me so much. Who I'm speaking to, is surely God. God is made of the things I have experienced, faces I have seen, and things I love. The grass and the sky. But also made of things I can't ever express and know by heart and will never know.

# Rickie Lee Jones Selected Discography

*Rickie Lee Jones* – 1979  (Warner Brothers Records)
*Pirates* – 1981  (Warner Brothers Records)
*The Magazine* – 1984 (Warner Brothers Records)
*Flying Cowboys* – 1989 (Geffen Records)
*Pop Pop* – 1991 (Geffen Records)
*Traffic From Paradise* – 1993 (Geffen Records)
*Naked Songs* – 1995 (Warner Brothers Records)
*Ghostyhead* – 1997  (Warner Brothers Records)
*It's Like This* – 2000 (Artemis Records)
*Live at Red Rocks* – 2001 (Artemis Records)
*Evening of My Best Day* – 2003 (V2 Records/BMG)

# THE PULSE OF THE COMMUNITY

## An Interview with Boots Riley

Preacher man wanna save my soul
Don't nobody wanna save my life
People we done lost control
Let's make heaven tonight
—from "Heven Tonite" by The Coup

A RAPPER for the Oakland, California band, The Coup, Boots Riley has followed in the footsteps of social-political hip hop bands like Public Enemy in his commitment to exposing the systems of exploitation and racism that he believes are destroying our society.

Boots was born as Raymond Riley on April 1, 1971 in Chicago. His father, who grew up in North Carolina during the Civil Rights movement, began working with the NAACP by the time he was in his early teens. He later worked with CORE (Congress on Racial Equality), the Progressive Labor Party, and members of the Black Panthers.

As a young person, Riley was a member of the youth activist groups, the Mau Mau Rhythm Collective and Young Comrades. At the age of fifteen, he helped organize effective community protests against racism in the Oakland school system and later challenged an anti-cruising law that was enforced by the Oakland police. The law was repealed by the Oakland City Council.

When he was eighteen, Riley witnessed police officers beating a woman and her twin eight-year-old sons at the Double Rock housing project in Oakland. As a crowd gathered to see what was going on, the police became nervous and fired shots into the air while attempting to make arrests. The crowd disrupted the arrests and the conflict grew more violent. By the end of the night, eight police cars had been turned over and the police officers had retreated without their guns, on foot. Riley was radicalized by the incident and it also gave him a firsthand look at how the local mainstream media cover such events. Not a word was mentioned in either of the local papers.

In the early 1990s his social activism was channeled into cofounding The Coup, which jumped onto the music scene in 1993 with their debut album, *Kill My Landlord*. The band is a collaboration between Boots Riley and Pam the Funkstress. Original member E-Rock left the group in 1997 to become a longshoreman. They have produced four albums: *Kill My Landlord* (1993), *Genocide and Juice* (1994), *Steal This Album* (1998), and *Party Music* (2001). *Party Music* was voted number one album of the year by the *Washington Post*, the *San Francisco Chronicle*, and *Time Out New York*.

Riley's loyalty lies with the underdog—with the single mother struggling to feed her children, with those who have suffered through the racist history of capitalism, and with the men and women from poor communities who fill the cells of the prison industrial complex. He advocates waking up to how things really are and turning things around with direct action. His belief in the power of people to organize and change their circumstances is offered in the song "Ghetto Manifesto" from the *Party Music* album:

> Even renowned historians have found that
> the people only bounce back when they pound back.

I met Boots Riley at his home in Oakland, California where the words "House of Music" are crafted on a metal gate in front of the house. Long before Riley bought the place, the recording studio inside had been the sight of numerous creative endeavors over the years. Riley cracked open the door to the studio, showing me the beginning stages of the remodel he is doing so he can use the space to make his new album. It will be the fifth studio album by The Coup and is scheduled for release in 2005 by Epitaph Records, who describe The Coup as "hardcore, communist-activist hip hop renegades."

In his distinctively low and gravelly voice, Riley spoke to me clearly and openly about his music and the feelings of compassion that drive him to work for a better world, while the sounds of the neighborhood drifted in. Next door, construction workers were hammering away and cars drove by with booming bass stereos. This is the neighborhood where his lyrics have been born, from stories of poverty, drugs, and confrontations with the police. His are stories of the possibilities for radical change that come through a commitment to seeing things as they really are and following a vision of what they can become.

Riley and The Coup remind us that the struggle for freedom is continuing to unfold and that any social revolution begins with a personal revolution and awakening of consciousness:

> Identify yourself, it's part of being conscious.
> If I call myself oppressed then I'm clear on where I'm at

sings Riley. Boots Riley and The Coup are shaking us, beckoning us to awaken and refresh our view so that we can manifest actions that contribute compassionately to our community.

▼ ▼ ▼ ▼ ▼

**John Malkin**: I once read that artists are like canaries in a coalmine for the societies they live in. That writers, painters, filmmakers, and musicians often alert the rest of the community to trouble or injustice. Is this how you view what you do with The Coup?

**Boots Riley**: I always take the position that the people who I am talking to already know what I am talking about. I am summing up. It is kind of like telling a good joke. When someone tells you a joke, they're not telling you something that you didn't already know. But it hits home because you never thought about it in that way before. I'm not Noam Chomsky researching secret meetings and deals and putting that into my music to give people brand new information. Maybe there is a need for that kind of music, but what I am doing is summing up experiences in a way that says, "Okay. It seems we should change things. What do you think?"

**JM**: One of the things I like about The Coup and your writing is the humor. Your song "Repo Man" goes into the song "Underdog" and goes from light and funny to very intense. What is the relationship of humor to making a serious point?

BR: Well, sometimes it is a very thin line and sometimes they are almost the same. I read Richard Pryor's autobiography, *Pryor Convictions*. A lot of the chapters start off with hilarious bits and then go into the actual events that are painful and horrifying. Humor lets us see how ridiculous the world is. If you can laugh at the world's craziness, you see that it is manageable. Nothing is too big to be ridiculed, and so nothing is too big to change.

Really, my political training came around a lot of folks that used humor. They just talked really funny and were very social people. I ended up being in the Progressive Labor Party, which was the same organization that my father had been in before. The main organizers were a couple of people from England who had really come up around trade union work in England and their whole attitude was, "You can't be an organizer if you don't drink!" You have to be in a bar with people, drinking and laughing and living and being a part of it all to be able to relate with them. A lot of times our conversations would include humor. Not just, "Let me make a funny joke about this," but just because as people, that is how we talk. So, I end up expressing a lot of my ideas that way, in everyday language. And as I got more comfortable with my art, then I put my everyday language into the music.

JM: In both politics and religion, often the founding ideals are lost somewhere along the journey. A separation develops between these initial ideals about making the world better and daily reality.

BR: I know that on my second album, *Genocide and Juice*, I had to make a conscious effort not to reference any revolutionaries and not to use the words "capitalism" or "communism." Because I really wanted to make sure that I understood the ideas I was talking about, much less everyone else understanding them. Sometimes general phrases and rhetoric stop us from understanding and take some of the life out of the things that we are going to say.

If every time someone talks about losing their job, I just pat them on the back and say, "It's the crisis of capitalism," it doesn't really explain anything. If that is the only thing that I can say, then I really don't understand what's going on. So, it is understanding things and getting a hold of what you actually believe in and what you don't that lets you play with these ideas. It is kind of like playing music. You can improvise a lot better if you know where all of the notes are and what something is going to sound like before you hit it.

But when you are just learning, you might be able to even copy a John Coltrane solo note for note because you practice it over and over, but you can't do your own solo. That is what it is all about. Getting in touch with what really is going on. Trying to understand it.

JM: It sounds as if you're talking about the idea of having structure and concepts, but only as a framework, not as rigid rules. And then you let go of the concepts in your life as you are living it.

BR: Yeah. On *Party Music*, our last album, I have a song called "Wear Clean Drawers," which is a song to my daughter. For a long time I resisted doing songs that were real personal because I felt like, "That is not really what I am in it for." But I had to trust myself and the fact that the things that I believe in, I really believe in, and they will come out in whatever I am talking about. What I believe is right and wrong will come out in everything that I do. So, the song came out. I did it and everyone is saying that it has feminist ideas in it. But really, it is just my ideas for what I want for my daughter, and what I would want for anybody.

JM: Tell me more about your father and how he became involved in political action and how he came out of the church doing that.

BR: Well, my father and his family are from Durham, North Carolina. My father's mother, at least, was very involved in one of the Holiness Churches where they speak in tongues. It was a fundamentalist church where I think she might have been called a saint. I don't exactly know.

At the age of twelve—I think this was in 1956—he stood up in church. Like a lot of kids, he had been very involved in the church. But he had read and heard about the Civil Rights movement, and he stood up in church and said he thought that they should be involved in this Civil Rights movement. That was what was happening right now, that was the right step and so on and so forth. That if the church wants to do good work, the Civil Rights movement was that work.

And the preacher went off against him, saying that he was blaspheming. That those were worldly affairs and how dare he bring that up in his church. But a lot of people may not know, even though the Civil Rights movement is portrayed as really being held up by black churches, that it was the exception for a black church to be involved in it. Many churches had the idea of keeping things the way they were.

So, the preacher said to my father: "Jesus wouldn't want you to do this," and my father said, "If Jesus doesn't want to help my people, then I don't want to have anything to do with him!" So, he left the church and the whole family got kicked out. And the whole family was a lot, back then! My father's family was twelve brothers and sisters. Not to mention cousins. It probably could've been half the town, I don't know. So, the family eventually got back in it, but he never did. He went and joined the NAACP and they didn't really have anyone in that area. So, he ended up being the southeast coordinator for the NAACP at the age of twelve or thirteen. Eventually, later on in the sixties, he joined CORE and then CORE moved him out here to the Bay Area. He went to San Francisco State and was involved in the San Francisco State strike and joined the Progressive Labor Party.

JM: What kind of effect did your father's political work have on your political life? I know that he ended up working with the Black Panthers. What has been your involvement with the Black Panthers?

BR: Well, my father ended up becoming a lawyer later on and he ended up representing David Hilliard and a few other Panthers after the Panthers were no longer together. I got involved in politics at the age of fourteen or fifteen. When I was fifteen, I helped lead a walkout at my high school about a prejudiced system. Twenty-one hundred students showed up *outside* the school and marched down to the school district building and we won a victory right then.

The principal, who was an ex-cop, went on a real big campaign of redbaiting. I remember one day after that, over the loudspeaker, the principal just decided to say, "We want to tell all of you students to not listen to Raymond Riley. He is a communist and wants to bring us back to the days of the Black Panthers." I didn't even know what the Black Panthers were. I knew their image, but I didn't know ideologically who they were.

Many other people at my school didn't know ideologically who they were either. There were even a few people who were named after Panthers, but they didn't know who these Panthers were. I remember certain kids coming up to me and saying that the Panthers were like a black Ku Klux Klan. You know? And this was Oakland, California, mind you, home of the Panthers just a few years before.

JM: Sometimes it seems like people think of political action and spirituality as very separate things. You described your father's experience when he was young, being in church and suggesting that the church get involved in the Civil Rights movement and the preacher saying, "No, that is worldly—we won't get involved in that." On the other hand, there are social change movements that have had a great impact on the world that have combined political action and spirituality. I think of Gandhi in India and Martin Luther King, Jr. here in the United States during the Civil Rights movement. How important do you think spirituality is in political action? What role has it played in your life? Is it revolutionary?

BR: First of all, let me explain something. I credit a lot of my artistic ability and my ability to speak to people about political ideas to the fact that from the time of eleven I have been like a door-to-door salesman. I was that kid who came up knocking at the door with the newspaper subscription trying to get you to get it. I was really good at it because I was able to take clues from what I could see about people and their houses and talk to them and see where they were at. I could say the things that they wanted to hear and get them to buy the paper. It was scary how good I was. And I always ended up having telemarketing jobs or something like that and I was always really good at it.

Once I had this fundraising job where I could come in on one day and make all the money I needed for one month and then go off and do whatever I wanted. But I felt empty and bad afterward. In my music, I use that same skill of focusing on what needs to be said. Here is an idea. I don't want to get caught up in these words. What is my connection to that idea?

I don't believe in God. But I believe that there is a connection between all things. What I do, even if nobody knows it, is important to the world. I wouldn't necessarily use the term "spiritual" for myself, but I think that's the same thing that people mean when they say that they are spiritual, I think they mean that they are in touch with the universe. And that is what I want to be. That is why I want to be involved with the world. Through being more in touch with the world, I am more alive. So, if I change things and help make someone's life easier, if I stop some sort of exploitation, I am putting out that good energy in a real way. For me, it's not enough just to think about the world and just to put out good energy and try to express goodness through your style of speaking. I think that energy has to manifest itself in the material.

Even a lot of people who don't call themselves spiritual who are involved in politics have this deep feeling of needing to do good things for other people. You know, part of that comes out of a drive to *be* connected. People want to feel: I was there. I mattered. My life is not just being lived in vain. A lot of times when people go on what they call a spiritual journey, it's similar. People don't want to just go through this life without understanding their connection to the universe.

I think that the best way of learning is through doing. You know? That is how you learn music. That's how you learn many things in science. So, you learn your connectedness by being with the universe, by being involved with the universe.

JM: It sounds like you really believe that people have some ability to make their lives connected and worthwhile and that we can make our communities and our whole world just and happy and peaceful. Maybe all religious and wisdom traditions have an original idea based in this belief. In Christianity there is the idea that the Kingdom of God is within you. Heaven is not going to happen later, after this life. If you want to make it happen, you are the one who is going to do it. In Buddhism there is a similar idea using the words, "The Pure Land is here and now." Your song "Heven Tonite" seems to have some of this same feel.

BR: The chorus says:

> Preacher man want to save my soul
> don't nobody want to save my life
> people we done lost control
> let's make heaven tonight.

The chorus and the verses are saying that me being involved in changing the world *is* my connection to eternity. Because whatever I do right here and now is not just right here and now! It will affect things forever. That's my connection to eternity. In a certain way, people think of the idea of heaven as, Okay, so you never die. Well, in a certain way, even if I am never conscious or whatever, I never die if I do something while I am here. You know? If I help people. Or make a change. Change the system so that what happens later is based on what I am doing right now.

I think that [spirituality and social change] are very connected. How am I realistically going to touch the universe? And that comes from the work that I do while I am here. It is also a criticism of a lot of organized religions that tell us that it doesn't really matter, we're going to be gone.

Somebody handed me this book one time and I leafed through it. I don't know if I have the right summation of what it was about, but the title gives you a good idea—it is called *Finite and Infinite Games*.[3] The book says that life is all a game and you can choose a finite game, which isn't going to matter because it all keeps going and you're going to be gone. Or you can get more in touch with yourself and choose an infinite game. It is basically all bullshit to go through life saying, "It doesn't matter. It is all going to be over with sometime. Let's just wait." Even if it is all going to be over with, what are you going to do? Or if it is going to keep going and it is infinite, are you just going to spend an eternity not doing anything? Just waiting for the next cycle or something like that? That would be more like hell to me then heaven. You know? You're just taking up space, cosmic space. You need to move over for people who are happy to be here or want to be involved.

I start out "Heven Tonite" like a prayer. But it is kind of more like my idea of my connectedness:

> Now as I sleep
> may the oxygen inflate my lungs
> may my arteries and heart oscillate as one.

And I take it to some more reality:

> If police come, may I awake, escape, and run
> and in the morning may I have the sake to scrape the funds.

3 James P. Carse, (New York: Ballantine, 1994).

There can be many names for it, but the questions still remain. What are you going to actually *do* to be connected to the universe? Are you hiding from reality or engaging in it?

JM: Some of your songs are about the lives of people in Oakland, California. Earlier I met someone who lives across the street, a sixty-nine-year-old retired man. He said that since the beginning of the year, and it is only March, fourteen people have been killed in this neighborhood. I don't know if he was exaggerating or if that is true. What is life like in this neighborhood?

BR: It is very loving and very family-oriented. There is one thing that I have to say about a lot of the so-called statistics. Especially dealing with Oakland. I have heard some general statistics about the U.S., but there is a whole thing going on, a campaign to bring more police. So, they keep talking about the number of people killed. And the number of people killed is actually going down every year. And compared to even in the sixties, it is way less.

The idea of change is not just, "Let's convince people to be more peaceful." Because that is not going to necessarily work. If you are selling weed and somebody just comes to your house and takes all of your weed and walks off with it and that is your way of surviving, that is how you're going to pay your rent for the next six months and you've got kids, there is going to be a fight. That is how it goes.

Often statistics criminalize the image of black youth. And then people believe all of the atrocities that are done to black youth are okay because these young people are considered criminal beings and immoral. In the sixties in Oakland, they banned the Blues because there were too many killings supposedly and the parents of the kids back then were saying, "The Blues are making our children crazy!"

It's an old story. In the twenties the media had a whole thing about how black youths were supposedly just on a rampage. They had police coming and going into people's houses and taking guns from them. The first gun control laws were designed to control black people.

JM: That reminds me that the Black Panthers walked around this area with guns and it was legal to do so at the time.

**BR**: And because of that, they took that right away. They don't enforce gun control in the white rural areas. The laws aren't going to stop anybody from getting guns or anything like that. It is similar to the laws around drugs. There are more white kids selling and using cocaine than black kids. There are more white kids selling and using crack than black kids, but by their arrest and jail records, you would assume the opposite. The gun control laws end up being used to criminalize black youth, to make it seem as if the problem is with the kids, not the system.

**JM**: *Party Music* was set to be released in October 2001. In August, ads ran with the cover depicting you and Pam standing in front of the World Trade Center blowing up the towers. A month later, on September 11, 2001, the World Trade Center was attacked, the towers were destroyed, and many people were killed. Subsequently, the U.S. government attacked Afghanistan and Iraq and now is occupying Iraq. People are probably going to ask you about this CD cover for the rest of your life. What was the original idea behind that cover and what did you feel when that image you'd created for the cover of *Party Music* became a reality on September 11th?

**BR**: Okay, when we made the album cover, the idea was to show that the goal of our music was to destroy capitalism. The music is symbolized in that picture by the bass guitar tuner I have in my hand and Pam's musical conductor's wands. So, whatever was going to be blowing up, it needed to be a symbol of capitalism. Well, it couldn't be the White House. That has been done already so many times. There are so many images in popular culture of the White House blowing up that nobody would even wonder or think about that. I also don't think that that's where the seat of power is. I don't think that the White House is where policy is actually decided. I think that that's where it is dispersed to the public, but the ruling class makes the decision in the same way that Enron and other companies made energy policy.

The World Trade Center was a symbol of capitalism because of all the commerce that went on there. Our image placement was similar to September 11th because, composition-wise, the planes had to be over our heads and in the top part of the buildings. A lot of people said, "It was in exactly the same place," but it was just in the top half of it.

When the towers were actually attacked on September 11th, it was hard to comprehend. First of all, we see those types of images in popular culture all of the time, so to see it on TV again really doesn't display to you the realness of it. We see war movies all of the time. It's not the same as being there. When people come back from war, they're traumatized and they are, many times, dysfunctional for the rest of their lives in some way, shape or form. But you see it on TV and it's, "Hey, those people just got blown up!" There is a big disconnect.

So, there was a disconnection. When I first heard that some planes ran into the World Trade Center, I didn't picture it as looking the same as the CD cover. I think only later when people started telling stories did I understand. It's an atrocity. All of these people are killed. It is a terrible thing. I think that as people started telling me their stories of "This was my father," or "This was my friend," it became real.

My friend Jeremy Glick's father was at the World Trade Center at the time and he died. Jeremy sent me an email afterwards and said, "The first thing I want you to do is to tell everyone that there should be no war for oil in our name." A group of families of the victims were saying this a few days after September 11th. But it got no press. They went to the White House with signs that said "No War In Our Name" and the *New York Times* put their picture in the paper but without the placards and the caption said, "Victims' families mourn their loss."

JM: Wow. That leaves out the whole message that they brought there.

BR: Exactly! And that was done to me a few times. *Rolling Stone* misquoted me on purpose. They didn't want me to get hate mail, so they quoted me saying that I had never advocated violent revolution. It was a totally fabricated quote. It wasn't like they left out a word. They added a word and put two sentences together from different parts. Later, they admitted it after a woman from the *Wall Street Journal* did an investigative report. And when I asked them to print a correction, they said, "No, but you can write a letter and we'll print it." [Laughter]

JM: What was it that you had actually said?

BR: They just asked me, "Has The Coup ever advocated violent revolution?" and I said, "Yes, but terrorism is much different. Revolution is something where there are hundreds of thousands, if not millions of people, just occupying facilities and the fight happens when the military of whoever's ruling comes and tries to fight you for it." They put in a thing that said, "The Coup doesn't really advocate violent revolution." [Laughter]

JM: What is your view on the strategy of nonviolence in social change and revolution?

BR: I think nonviolence is a tactic. I just don't rule out all tactics. To let people starve and not do what you can to stop that from happening, that's a form of violence.

This system—capitalism—is based on an inequity. By design. So no matter how good people become inside that system, no matter how good a heart some head of a corporation may have, he can only work within that system. And the only way to stop that is through actually reclaiming certain things. There ends up, sometimes, being a fight.

Joe Hill said that really the revolution could happen if everyone at lunch just took off, had a picnic, and came back and said, "Everything is going to be different now." That takes organization. And people physically fight you to not be able to organize in the first place.

I think that there would be no trade unions if they had a nonviolent philosophy. The whole philosophy behind a strike is: "We're not working and you better not try to send somebody else in here to work. And that is how we are going to get higher wages." If trade unions had a nonviolent philosophy, everybody would still be working eighteen-hour days in the United States, which they are in other places because they don't really have trade unions. Trade unions only happened through people saying: "This is what we're doing and you're physically not able to stop us because there are more of us than you!" And the whole idea that "there are more of us than you" is a *violent* idea. Because what does it matter if there are more of us than you if we're going to just let you walk all over us?

JM: You are saying that there is some force that is available when you have that intention. I suppose that you could call it violent. It is a fine line between what is violent and what is nonviolent. But, these tactics that you are describing of striking and "we are more than you" were held by Martin Luther King, Jr. and Gandhi as the most important strategy of *nonviolence*. Martin Luther King, Jr. was beginning to organize a nationwide strike.

BR: Well, in the end, Martin Luther King, Jr. said of the Vietcong, "They are freedom fighters." You know? He went that far. But to have a strike really be successful, you can't just let scabs come in. "Okay, we're going to have a strike at the plant, but whoever wants to come in, we're not going to stop you." You know? Because at some point they start pushing and you start pushing back. There is force applied. Now, you could say tactically, "I don't want to have my hand move really fast into someone's head." You could say, "I don't want to do that." But either way, it is some sort of violence. You could say, "We don't want violence because that makes a different thing happen." That is using physical force, either way. If you're stopping someone from coming in, it is using physical force to stop someone. I am down with those sorts of things. Martin Luther King, Jr. and Gandhi both relied on the media. Because one idea behind nonviolence is that you'll bring shame on your aggressors. But this only works if the media pays attention and reports fairly. So, the tactics that we choose cannot be based on the assumption that the world will know what we're doing. Because it won't.

JM: Some people think that the only way to get media attention is to do something violent.

BR: I disagree with the tactics of some of the anarchist groups. While I think their ideas come out of frustration with a lot of the movements that are going on, I think they miss the point that you *bring the people with you*. Right? Everybody is eating at McDonald's or everybody is drinking at Starbucks. Starbucks has a certain class thing to it, so let's say everybody is eating at McDonald's and you think that McDonald's is doing something wrong. Breaking out the windows at McDonald's is only going to make people say, "Damn, I can't come in here now."

The point of organizing is having your finger on the pulse of the community. What are the things and issues that are going to get people mobilized? But many times, many organizations decide on the problem, and organize around it without working with the community. The opposition to the World Trade Organization is an example. The sentiment is correct and the analysis of what the WTO does is correct, but where is the movement around housing and around higher wages?

JM: In the sixties and seventies the FBI infiltrated organizations that were working for peace and justice. The FBI and police killed activists. Martin Luther King, Jr. was spied on by the FBI. Black Panthers were killed and their office in Oakland was attacked. Now we live in a time when maybe it is not so clear what kind of programs the government is involved in, but the Patriot Act has passed and people are very concerned about civil rights. Do you think that it is difficult to be radical and active now, to be speaking the truth? Is it a difficult time?

BR: No. Actually, because of everything that is going on, just average everyday people are more in tune politically. There is no way that you could ever hope to hide from the FBI or anything like that, so your organizing campaigns have to be out in the open anyway. So there is no reason for them to really even spy on what you're doing. Whatever I say on the phone, I am going to say in front of 50,000 people. There is no surprise.

You can't organize for justice covertly. The whole point is to create a movement in which the people know they're involved in bringing about change. And when the people are involved in campaigns that make change, they know when they've had a victory or can learn from a loss.

JM: What do you think about the relationship between social justice movements and hip hop and if there is any relationship between spiritual movements and hip hop.

BR: With hip hop, or music in general, if there is an idea in the music and you're listening to it and you know a crowd of other people are listening to it, you automatically feel a sense of a unity. You know that there are other people who like that song and you get this sense that you are not alone.

I think with church, a lot of times people are going to feel like they're a part of something. Either the congregation or a part of the world and the universe, and their lives are never going to end. There is a similar feeling that comes with listening to music. You feel connected and the ideas that are being expressed are shared by many people.

# Boots Riley Selected Discography

*Kill My Landlord* – 1993 (Wild Pitch)

*Genocide & Juice* – 1994 (Wild Pitch)

*Hip Hop Meets West* Compilation Album – 1997 (Priority Records)

*Steal This Album* – 1998 (Dogday Records)

*No More Prisons* Compilation Album – 2000 (Raptivism)

*Stray From the Pack* Compilation Album – 2000 (Stray Records)

*Party Music* – 2001 (75 Ark Entertainment)

*Steal This Double Album* – 2002 (Foad Records)

# WAKING UP

AN INTERVIEW WITH MICHELLE SHOCKED

Jealousy and anger
Greed and hypocrisy
The seasons of human nature
Cannot take my joy from me
Joy, joy, joy, hallelujah!
—from "Can't Take My Joy" by Michelle Shocked

MICHELLE SHOCKED was born in East Texas in 1962, in the same neck
of the woods that had produced blues artists like Freddie King, Leadbelly,
and Gatemouth. In 1977, she ran away from her Christian Evangelical
mother to live with her father, who introduced her to folk and blues music.
She spent the early 1980s in Austin, Texas, writing and playing her music.

She attended the University of Texas in Austin for a while and, as she puts
it, "the strain led to a little postgrad work in the Baylor Hospital psych ward."
Later, she traveled to New York and Europe where she says she "pursued a
masters degree in Street Studies with a focus on pirate radio, squatting,
poetry, anti-fascism, feminism, rape, socialism, and green anti-apartheid punk
anti-nuclear anarchist philosophy. It was alright, but I got homesick."

In 1986, Shocked was volunteering at the Kerrville Folk Festival in Texas,
when Pete Lawrence recorded her singing and telling stories. Lawrence didn't
mention at the time that he was a partner in a new independent British record
label. Without her knowledge, the recording of Shocked was released by
Cooking Vinyl Records later that same year, with the title, *The Texas Campfire
Tapes*. The record became a surprise hit, moving to the top of the independent charts in Britain.

Shocked first learned of the record when she was in New York, a few months after being recorded in Kerrville. A friend who had recently returned from Amsterdam gave her a magazine that included a flexi-disc of a song called "Who Cares?" by Michelle Shocked. Shocked was not only unaware that her music had been distributed, but she couldn't remember ever having written a song with that title. Things became clear when she placed the disk on the turntable and heard her own voice introducing the song, "This is my most recent song and it's called... oh, who cares!"

*The Texas Campfire Tapes* became her debut recording and was aired repeatedly on the BBC. Shocked played her first show at London's Queen Elizabeth Hall. Soon after, Shocked took the risk of signing with Mercury, a major label, with the idea that she would change the corporate recording industry from within. She maintained ownership of her music by turning down the label's advance and she decided to organize her songs into a trilogy of LPs that would illustrate her musical roots. *Short, Sharp, Shocked* was a picker poet album, followed by an upbeat blues album titled *Captain Swing*. The third album, *Arkansas Traveler*, was "recorded on steamboats, in barns, log cabins, and even recording studios."

It was in South Central Los Angeles that Shocked was inspired to take a new direction, both spiritually and artistically. After twenty years of estrangement from organized religion, she began attending the Sunday morning services at the West Angeles Church of God in Christ, one of LA's largest African American churches. Her first visits there were to listen to the choir, but she soon realized that she'd become a "bona fide Pentecostal born-again Christian, despite the glaring contradictions of its socially conservative doctrine."

Shocked decided to record an album of prayers that she'd composed, but Mercury refused to fund the project and blocked her efforts to have other labels produce the work. They refused to renegotiate her contract and from 1993 to 1996, Shocked toured worldwide, playing 238 performances. *Kind Hearted Woman* came out of that period, an album that was independently produced and sold only at shows. In 1995, she was released from her contract when she initiated a lawsuit that cited a violation of her civil liberties under the Thirteenth amendment, which prohibits slavery. Later, BMG released a second version of *Kind Hearted Woman*. Today, she is likely the only known major label artist to own and publish her own catalog.

She has been active in opposing the U.S. government's war in Iraq and in supporting grassroots organizations like Code Pink, ANSWER's antiwar coalition, the Dennis Kucinich for President campaign, and the Christian-based organization, Save Africa's Children.

Michelle has recently expanded her medium of communication by publishing a self-edited magazine called *Jams*. The first issue includes an article by Clarence Gatemouth Brown, a piece titled "Bush and the Rise of Christian Fascism," an interview with Taj Mahal, and an essay by Michelle that says, "I never planned on a music career. My choice had been activism. Trouble is, I'm not a very talented activist. However, in my pursuit of activism, seeds of a vision were planted in my mind…and here is my vision: I see this country as a penal colony. One class of people own the prison, and it turns a profit. A managing class, like prison guards, works for them. Another class of people, perhaps not you, are the warehoused prison stock." She adds that "change won't come from a leader, but rather, from people who think for themselves."

When Michelle Shocked emphatically states, "I want to change the world," I believe her. Her art and social activism are interwoven. She has always been willing to challenge the corporate control of the music recording industry and courageous enough to follow her own vision as it changes and transforms. Her independent thinking and outspoken criticism against racism have paved the way for other artists to challenge institutions of oppression and build social systems that are based on autonomy and compassion.

▼ ▼ ▼ ▼ ▼

**John Malkin**: It is such a joy to watch you perform. You look like you are really enjoying yourself.

**Michelle Shocked**: It's nice to not have to go through the motions. I have managed to preserve a great deal of integrity, you know, with what I do and with what I say I do. I have found that life is a lot more enjoyable that way! There was a time I remember when I was being overworked, early on, and people were telling me things like, "Go as far as you can 'cause it is all going to be down hill from here." I thought, "Man, I am not going to be doing the best work of my life in the first few years. It is just going to keep getting better as I get older." I try to pace myself so that I really enjoy it. And I really love my band.

JM: You put out a lot of love and joy. You seem to sing about looking into pain and seeing healing, looking into the dark and seeing light, and looking into ugliness and seeing beauty. This seems to be the real stuff that your music and you are made of.

MS: It is hard to articulate and shape that experience into words—being able to see beauty in ugliness, being able to see light in darkness—those are all of the poetic devices that one can use to describe how you can see the unseen. I didn't used to be that way. I used to be unable to see the forest for the trees. And now I know, even when I am staring at one tree trunk, that there is a whole beautiful forest standing behind it. Maybe that is bland, too. I don't know how to say it! The nut of it is, trying to articulate faith, that process whereby a person can do the impossible, see the invisible. That is where I come from these days.

JM: It sounds like recognizing the largeness and the love that is bigger than you—this human mind and human body—there is something larger that is coming through you.

MS: That is my faith. My prayer every day is "use me." Use me. I know what I would do with my life if I was running things and planning the show. But time and time again—I can't tell you how many times in my life—I have had to learn the hard way that I am clearly not in charge. And the best that I can hope for is that all of the experiences that I have, all of the opportunities that present themselves to me—even though I may be thinking that I am creating it or taking it—it's being given to me like a gift.

Again, we are trying to articulate that stuff: Life is a gift. Without faith, it is really easy to forget that. I had just gotten into that very dark place where I was literally wishing that I'd never been born. I couldn't seem to do any good. Now I've gone one hundred and eighty degrees the other way! It wasn't even that hard. It was in a simple, gentle way. I don't know! I just hope that people who listen to this aren't saying, "Oh Lord, there they go again!"

JM: A lot of people have prejudices about a certain religious vocabulary. There are some good reasons for that; religion has developed into some pretty negative stuff. But the basis of all religions is truth, love, and compassion, and, to a large extent, about giving yourself over to this joy that is larger than just us.

MS: Yeah. This is something that you can kind of wander through for many, many years. The bottom line is that I am a stone cold Christian. Me, of all people! And there is a lot of baggage that comes with that particular ideology. And a lot of people try to get around it by just seeing what the good things in Christianity have in common with all of the great spiritual faiths of the world. For me personally there was a very gentle and natural process that took place, whereby I realized, "Oh my goodness! What are people going to think of this one?"

I had to let it go. Coming to religion wasn't what I would have planned for myself. That's a fact. But at least I had the courage and the integrity when it happened to go with it. And it is leading me to some very, very interesting places.

JM: What do you think is the role of faith, religion, or spirituality in social change?

MS: That is the most common paradigm that people understand; either you can be for this world or you can be against this world. A lot of Christian theology has to do with saying that this world is not our home, this world is not what matters. It's all about the next life. And a lot of social activists are frustrated with that idea because it doesn't address the very unpleasant ugly realities of what goes on in social injustices.

Maybe I can explain my perspective through a very personal experience I had. I got a tour bus this year and it has really made my life better on the road to have a home. The good side of the tour bus is that you can have a very personalized experience traveling from place to place. The bad part about a tour bus is that it is always breaking down! So, imagine, about a month ago, the engine completely blew out on my bus. And I was in the middle of nowhere—except, where a lot of people live. Which is to say it broke down in Bristol, Tennessee. Bristol. It is half Tennessee, half Virginia. And within ten minutes of the tow truck arriving I had already been informed that Bristol has a, what did they say, a "two percent minority rate."

What happens for me is that I feel I am being sown like a seed is sown. I would not have planned this for myself. But I stayed willing and open and had faith that this breakdown in Bristol was not perfectly meaningless. What has been changing and going on in my life makes a kind of sense, when I have the luxury of stepping back and looking at it.

I found myself, that Sunday morning in Bristol, accepting an invitation to go with some residents to Mount Zion Baptist Church. And let's just say, 11:00 AM Sunday morning is the most segregated hour in America. If all of these brotherly-loving Christians can't even get it together to break down racism and segregation, what hope do the rest of us heathens have? For me, the beauty is that there is so much to work with and work to do. Whether you call yourself an activist or a Christian or any kind of religious person, I don't really care what you call it. But there is such a wide swath of work to do when you are walking between worlds. Some people decide, "Okay, that's not for me. I am going to stay around my own kind. People who think like me, dress like me, act like me." But for me, I am much happier putting myself in a position where I can see more than one point of view.

I can do a pleasant show. I don't have to be up there spouting off the polemics of this and that. But if George W. Bush thinks he's going to war in Iraq without me having a thing to say about it, he's got another thing coming!

I just have that sense that there is a power, there is a force behind my individual actions, even though on a small scale it looks like what I'm doing is absolutely irreconcilable and ludicrous.

JM: The cover of *Short, Sharp, Shocked* is a photograph of you being held in a chokehold by a San Francisco cop. What was the purpose of that cover?

MS: I like to think of it as a prototype of the WTO anti-globalization movement. Because we were protesting corporations who had contributed to both the Democratic and Republican campaigns in 1984. That photo was taken of course in San Francisco in front of a company owned by Diamond Shamrock. Our criteria wasn't *just* that they had contributed money to both parties, thereby effectively buying our democracy, but also that they had profiteered in some way from the cold war policies that were going on at that time. I knew that the photo existed because it had appeared with the story of the protest.

I kind of slept through the Clinton years. I knew going into it that centrism was going to be the death of us all. But I had to experience it for myself. So,

I slept through the Clinton years and I am slowly waking up from a long sleep and realizing...I really am grateful for the groundwork that has been laid by the anti-globalization movement because it is going to give a lot of people a lot of tools to empower themselves within the coming years. Very exciting times.

**JM**: Do you have any thoughts about the attacks of September 11th and the subsequent invasion in Afghanistan, the larger invasion in Iraq, and all the new security measures?

**MS**: You can look at what happened on September 11th as an act of war or as a crime against humanity. And therein lies the rub. Whichever road you go down, you're going to enjoy the fruits of that choice. Obviously, I am inclined and disposed to see it as something that affects all of humanity. It is something all of humanity can speak out about and address.

I certainly don't give Americans any special privilege. By that I mean, folks have been kind of willing to shoulder the idea that we have to sacrifice liberties for securities. And again, this wasn't me but Thomas Jefferson who said, "Those who sacrifice liberty for security deserve neither." I am of that ilk.

I just have been reading the *No Nonsense Guide to Free Trade* and *The No Nonsense Guide to Democracy*. Reading that stuff has brought me up to speed after a long slumber.

**JM**: You have a song on your CD *Deep Natural* called "Forgive to Forget." The liner notes read, "Let it go, let it go, let it go—repeat until it's true." Is this your idea of forgiveness?

**MS**: That is how I see it. Forgiveness is a power greater than love. And there has been *so* much said on the power of love, to the point of nausea. Love is a great power, but like anything else, you beat it to death and it loses its potency. I think that forgiveness has such an amazing power because it is one that we possess when we are at our weakest. When we've been wronged, hurt, injured, betrayed, let down, or disappointed, our instinct is to lash out in anger and pain because we feel so powerless.

And I wrote the song to remind myself, really. Because I can't always practice what I preach. It is at that moment when we're at our weakest, that we have the choice to exercise a power greater than love. What could be better than that? Forgiveness does not rely on the other person coming to us and saying, "I wronged you. I caused you injury and pain." Forgiveness calls upon us to recognize the source of peace that is within all of us.

JM: I never knew the origins of the song "Amazing Grace." You mentioned it tonight.

MS: John Newton [the author of the song] was a slave trader in the 1880s who had one of those kind of Paul-on-the-road-to-Damascus experiences. I think "Amazing Grace" is such a great folk song. For a song to survive in such a powerful way, it has to have a powerful genesis to it. That is why I love gospel music. I say it's the greatest folk music being practiced today!

JM: How do you manage to produce and own your own music? Or maybe I should ask, "How do other musicians *not* manage to do that?"

MS: I hope that I can explain this one succinctly. It has to do with the Western tradition of property rights. Long ago, intellectual property rights were established by creators—writers, photographers, choreographers, etc. But because the technology of recording was relatively new, it established a practice early on that treated the creators as hired hands. It assumed that artists in a recording studio weren't creating, they were being told what to create. That isn't true. But it really had to do, once again, with the balance of power over who owned and controlled the technology versus those being brought to employ it. And I think that the biggest problem is that there never has successfully been the ability to create a powerful guild or a union for these particular types of creators. There is AFTRA, the union for recording and television artists, and there is the Federation of Musicians, but they don't do enough.

How I chose to approach it when I went into the negotiation was to say that my songs, my talents, were my natural resources, not intellectual property. It's the same thing that happens on the international scale. If Brazil hadn't gotten into debt, it wouldn't have then had to subsequently cut down its rainforest. So, I didn't take the money up front. On the advice of a slightly older artist named Nanci Griffith, I put my stake in ownership of my master recordings.

Now dig this! Here is the real point. These labels, they are so blatant in their abuse of power that even though I had finally, for the first time as an artist, negotiated a contract that was reasonable and fair to artists, they still ten years later came back and employed tactics designed to basically force me to renegotiate the terms. I was perfectly happy with the deal that I had negotiated! They would let me go in and record, but they wouldn't let me leave and go record for anyone else. So, they were basically saying, "You want a career? You have to play ball our way." I just stood on the principle, and on the shoulders of artists who had come before me.

I had spent enough time in the Bay Area around the scene that surrounded the magazine *Maximum Rock'N'Roll* that I had some idea of what was going on. I always thought of myself as having worked outside the system. But here I was beginning to go into the system to try and change it. I didn't go into the system thinking, "Oh, they're going to be nice and treat me different." I thought, "Well, I don't know where my battle is going to lie, but I am going to go in there and find a battle to fight." Again, it wasn't what I had planned for myself, but I really think that I struck a very, very righteous blow on behalf of the artists who create music. And whether it will change in my lifetime or not, I don't know, but I can tell you this—I helped set a precedent.

I don't know any other artist who's in quite as unique a position as I am. But let it be said, too, I was sort of cocky going in because I had had this phenomenon take place where this guy had recorded me on his tape recorder and released it as a record. So, the major labels had come knocking on my door. I had never gone to them saying, "Please, please, please, please! Please, can I create beauty?"

**JM**: That is great luck, great timing, and great talent.

**MS**: Do you see why I have faith now? This is a beautiful thing that I can look back on now and say, "Hey, if I was God, wouldn't this be a cool way to play this one off?" You know, have a little—what's that phrase—a little troublemaker just sitting in the wings waiting to be pulled out whenever there's things that need to be addressed.

JM: Do you get a mixed response when you talk about God or about faith when you play in different towns?

MS: No. Because I keep it very light. I used to tour with Billy Bragg. Now, there is a man who has no problem preaching to the converted! Here is my philosophy as a performer: I don't think that anything I have to say on a stage is nearly as important as my ability to draw together a community who are now standing in a common space, looking each other in the eye, and saying, "Oh, is this how you think about something? Well, this is how I think." And sharing their points of view. I don't consider myself necessarily a spokesperson, but I am perfectly willing to be the host of a really fun party.

JM: You convey more than information or ideas. You convey a feeling of joy.

MS: Thank God. I am glad it is somewhat unique. Because I have pretty much determined that I am otherwise unemployable!

# Michelle Shocked Selected Discography

*Texas Campfire Takes* – 1986/2003 (Mercury Records/Mighty Sound)
*Short Sharp Shocked* – 1988/2003 (Mercury Records/Mighty Sound)
*Captain Swing* – 1989/2004 (Mercury Records/Mighty Sound)
*Arkansas Traveler* – 1992/2004 (Mercury Records/Mighty Sound)
*Kind Hearted Woman* – 1994 (Private Music)
*Artists Make Lousy Slaves* with Fiachna O'Braonain – 1996 (Mood Swing)
*Mercury Poise: 1988-1995* – 1996 (Mercury Records)
*Good News* with the Anointed Earls – 1998 (Mood Swing)
*Dub Natural* – 2001 (Mood Swing)
*Deep Natural* – 2002 (Mighty Sound)

# COMMON GROUND

## AN INTERVIEW WITH DARRYL CHERNEY

I'm the man that they call Jesus Christ, you may remember me well
In the year number one I took my life in my hands
And brought faith to a world to make way for the rest
And they formed a religion to carry my name
But the people forgot all the reasons I came
The warfare and hatred have followed with time
And when people say they are Christians
Do they really believe they are people of mine?
—from "Take Away My Name" by Darryl Cherney

ON MAY 24, 1990, I was looking forward to a visit to Santa Cruz by musician/activist Darryl Cherney and his colleague, Judi Bari. The two were scheduled to perform at the University of California in Santa Cruz that evening, to generate interest in the upcoming Earth First! Redwood Summer campaign, a season-long period of nonviolent direct actions to save the giant redwood forest of northern California.

Cherney and Bari never made it to Santa Cruz that night. Their journey was violently interrupted in Oakland, when a pipe bomb exploded in Bari's station wagon. Cherney was injured, and Bari nearly killed. Within fifteen minutes of the explosion, FBI agents were on the scene, accusing the pair of being domestic terrorists who had been wounded by their own bomb when it accidentally detonated.

It would take eleven years to find some legal resolution to the matter, but on June 11, 2002, a unanimous jury verdict determined that the FBI and Oakland Police Department had violated the First and Fourth Amendments when they arrested Bari and Cherney for bombing themselves and did not investigate who actually had planted the bomb. The jury awarded Cherney and the family of Judi Bari (who had died of cancer in 1997) $4.4 million dollars. It was largest civil rights award ever declared regarding an FBI attack on a political group. After the trial, Cherney said that "the FBI itself is a threat to national security: not because they are a bunch of thugs—which they are—but because the FBI isn't capable of solving crimes."

Cherney even got a chance to sing for the jury during the court proceedings against the FBI and Oakland Police Department when an attorney for the FBI cross-examined him, attempting to draw a connection between Cherney and acts of violence. Though his attorney, Dennis Cunningham, was worried about the court performance, Cherney's singing of "Spike a Tree for Jesus" didn't seem to sway the jury out of his favor. And it was a true exhibit of the blend of humor, truth, music, and activism for which Darryl Cherney is so well-known.

The non-hierarchical, decentralized, autonomous, self-organized character of Earth First! has influenced the development of social change projects worldwide, like Indymedia centers and the current movements resisting the global-corporatization being carried forward by the World Trade Organization, the World Bank and others. Though Earth First! is "by nature and tradition a nonviolent movement," explains Cherney, they have advocated "monkey wrenching," a strategy of disrupting the corporate industrial machine by damaging logging equipment, for example, that was inspired by Edward Abbey's book, *The Monkeywrench Gang*.

Darryl Cherney was raised in New York City and graduated from Fordham University in 1977 with an M.S. in Urban Education. He volunteered on the presidential campaigns of John Lindsay and John Anderson, but was more focused on playing guitar with a variety of country and folk-rock bands in the 1970s. He worked briefly for United Artists records, promoting disco releases, but became disillusioned with the corporate music business. In 1985, he decided to move to California. He had been to the redwoods of California with his parents when he was fourteen and had always dreamed of living among them.

In Oregon, he stopped to give a ride to a man walking in the rain. While they drove, the man asked Cherney, "What do you want from life?" Cherney said he wanted to learn to live off the land and save the world. The man recommended that he go to Garberville, California, to the Environmental Protection Information Center.

In 1986, one year after moving to California, Cherney cofounded the Headwaters Forest Campaign with activist/photographer Greg King. He has helped to organize hundreds of Earth First! protests, rallies, and direct actions, involving thousands of acts of civil disobedience. His efforts have played a major role in protecting a number of forests, including the Headwaters Forest, Trout Creek, and the Cahto Wilderness in northern California.

Cherney has also confronted corporate destruction of forests by advocating litigation to enforce California's environmental protection laws and by legally challenging the practices of timber companies. He worked with Judy Bari to help activists and timber workers organize to meet their mutual needs, rather than work against each other. Cherney later brought together the United Steelworkers of America and Earth First! activists in a cooperative struggle against the MAXXAM corporation. He is a founding member of the Alliance for Sustainable Jobs and the Environment.

Throughout his work for environmental justice and civil rights, Cherney has continued to cultivate his songwriting and guitar-playing skills, creating passionate songs about the struggle to protect the Earth. He has released five independently produced albums. In 1997, Cherney created Environmentally Sound Promotions, a nonprofit organization with the motto, "Music, Arts, and Media for the Earth."

In the liner notes from his latest album, *Real American*, Cherney refers to Jesus as a "Jewish hippie peace activist who said you can't get into heaven if you own more than one robe." He also explains the true sense of what it means to be a real American: "We've got a real problem in this country and in the world. We've been surrounded by a pentagon of oppression—technology, religion, the military, the schools, and the communications network….We—all of us—are being dumbed down, hypnotized, poisoned, bombed, imprisoned, tortured, and just plain outright killed. But there's good news! We have the honor and the privilege of potentially being the last generation to be able to fight for life on this planet as we know it. That is the mission of a real warrior. And the mission of a real American."

▼ ▼ ▼ ▼ ▼

**John Malkin**: I want to start by asking you about May 24, 1990. I remember being here in Santa Cruz waiting for you and Judi Bari to arrive for a performance. What happened in Oakland on your way here?

**Darryl Cherney**: We were just leaving Oakland to go pick up the banjo player. I got into Judi Bari's car and we were following another car belonging to a Seeds of Peace member and within a few minutes, just before 12:00 noon, a bomb went off underneath Judi Bari's seat. It was a motion-triggered pipe bomb and it almost killed her. It fractured her pelvis. It shattered her coccyx and sacrum and caused intestinal damage. By some miracle, I was only slightly injured. A few minutes after the bombing the FBI showed up on the scene and, virtually instantaneously, the FBI and the Oakland police blamed us for bombing ourselves or for carrying a bomb that went off accidentally. Even though, of course, we were nonviolent activists on our way to a musical tour.

**JM**: What did the FBI and law enforcement people say to you when they arrived there on the scene?

**DC**: The FBI didn't say anything to me personally, at first, but the paramedics were exceedingly rude. That was my first inkling that something was wrong. Clearly, they had been told that we were bad guys. In the hospital the FBI first asked me who could have bombed us. This is about two or three hours after the bombing. I gave them a little laundry list of timber industry people who had been sending us death threats or encouraging violence against us. They just waved their hands and one of them said, "Look, we can tell if this is your bomb. Why don't you confess? Make it easy on all of us and get it over with."

**JM**: After that bombing, the media represented Earth First! as a violent organization and you were held on a $100,000 bail. To what extent was Earth First! committed to nonviolence? What do nonviolence and nonviolent direct action mean to you?

**DC**: Well, Earth First! is not really an organization so we don't have a formal set of bylaws. We don't have members, we have activists. We did come to a consensus at the 1990 activist conference that Earth First! was comprised of three components. The first being that we ascribe to biocentrism—that the biology of the planet must be at the center of our concerns and that all species have a right to be here for their own sake regardless of their value to human beings. The second principle is no compromise in defense of Mother Earth. And the third principle is to take some form of action.

Earth First! also has a set of traditions. We have a tradition of nonviolence. From the very first rendezvous I went to, people were giving nonviolence trainings and I have never been to an Earth First! encampment or action that didn't have a nonviolence code. However, there is nothing formally written on a piece of paper that says we are nonviolent, but our actions themselves have been nonviolent over the years.

Here is my definition of nonviolence and how it relates to Earth First!. We will be open and friendly to all people. We will not engage in violence, either verbal or physical. We will carry no weapons. We will observe fire danger. Earth First! added that to the nonviolence code a long time ago, to prevent violence to the Earth, especially during our summer actions. And we will use no illegal drugs or alcohol.

The last part of my personal code, which a lot of people might question as far as Earth First! goes, is that we will not destroy property. As an over-all philosophy, I think it is safe to say that Earth First! does feel, maybe collectively, that the destruction of equipment that is destroying the Earth is an act of self-defense and not, in and of itself, a violent act. Many feel that it is impossible to commit a true act of violence against an inanimate object.

The people in Plowshares for example, the Christian peace activists, are very honorable people who go to jail for as long as twenty years for break-ing into nuclear weapons facilities and destroying the machinery there. And the Wobblies [the members of the Industrial Workers of the World] and other unions sabotaged equipment for years. So, I don't think necessarily that being categorically against property destruction has to be part of a non-violence code. On the other hand, Earth First! has been strictly nonviolent towards human beings. We have never injured a single person in our twenty-four year history. I will let the people judge as to whether they regard the destruction of dangerous machinery as violent or not.

**JM:** The Plowshares movement you mentioned as well as the Catholic Workers and Mohandas Gandhi's movement in India and Martin Luther King, Jr. during the Civil Rights movement all based their work in spirituality. To what extent has your own work been connected to spirituality and ideas about how living beings are interconnected on this planet?

**DC:** My work is completely immersed in my spirituality. My spirituality is my work and my work is my spirituality. I am a pagan. Paganism to me is a generic term ascribed to spiritualities that honor the mother as well as the father. Earth Mother is sacred. And of course, it is possible for certain pagan practices to honor different spirits. Some people call them gods with a small "g," but I don't necessarily think that these words are important except that many of the Earth Firsters I know practice some form of honoring the Earth on some spiritual level. I think this spirituality is absolutely essential for any movement to be successful. Activists in many quarters have made a great mistake in shunning spirituality. The movements you've mentioned, and many more—including movements that oppose us, like the anti-abortion rights movement—are based in their own concept of spirituality. Some people in the Muslim world are fighting America now with a complete sense of spirituality behind them. And regardless of what your opinion is of any of these groups, when you operate from a spiritual place, you come with a much stronger conviction and, I would say, a willingness to offer your life. That doesn't mean that I or anybody in Earth First! is willing to take a life. That is the job of a soldier. But we are warriors and warriors offer their lives. This is why so many Earth Firsters sit in trees for up to two years at a time or are willing to stand in front of bulldozers and risk getting killed that way. David Gypsy Chain was killed when a logger felled a tree on him. We consider that the peril that the Earth is in is something worth risking our lives for in a very honoring way.

**JM:** On your latest CD, *Real American*, there is a song called "Take Away My Name." It includes verses about Henry Hudson, George Washington, and Jesus Christ. These people's actions and ideas have over time been changed and reorganized into something new that they themselves might not approve of. A lot of bloodshed has happened due to religious conflicts and over ideas about God. Christianity is a religion that was created in the name of Jesus

Christ, whose nonviolent teachings of loving your enemy and turning the other cheek are often forgotten in contemporary life. What was the impetus behind this song?

DC: That song is probably the oldest song that I've written that I still sing. I wrote it in 1975 or 1974, when I was eighteen or nineteen. So, it has a kind of innocence and even a political naiveté to it, in the way that I honor Henry Hudson and George Washington, who of course were not exactly angels. But these people are honored by most Americans in the mainstream society. The song comes from a younger, more innocent version of myself and yet at the same time my burgeoning, radical roots were emerging.

Jesus actually appears in every single one of my albums, on multiple occasions. Judi Bari used to call me a closet Christian. My latest album references Jesus in four songs. I call Jesus "the original Jewish hippy peace activist." To have his work distorted as a justification for war is very disconcerting to me. It should be a warning to all of us. Whatever we do can be co-opted and turned into something perverted if we don't lay the foundation properly.

I think the message of Jesus Christ is, "You can do a lot of great work in this world, but after you're dead you better have set up some kind of organizing, some kind of infrastructure in a good way." To me the message is also that really each one of us has to be our own Jesus Christ. Whatever Jesus had to say, other human beings are not going to be able to imitate that. When you record something that somebody says, especially on a cassette for example, there is a little bit of static on the second copy. If you pass that down to another generation, there is a little bit more static and then a little more static. I think that we have gotten to the point with Christianity that all we hear is the static and we don't hear the original message. So, each one of us has to be our own savior. For me, this is part of the philosophy of being a righteous human being on planet Earth, whether you call it anarchism, Christianity, Buddhism, or something else.

JM: What role has anarchism played in your activism and your social change work?

DC: I consider myself a tribalist. For me, the anarchist movement of late doesn't necessarily resemble the anarchist movement of old. And I am not quite sure what anarchism is. For me, the reason I resonate with tribalism is because it is the natural order of human affairs. If we take a look at how human beings acted and the kind of social structure we created when we were living in harmony with nature—when we were just another one of the animals roaming the planet—human beings were like a herd animal. We traveled in small groups of thirty or so and followed certain traditions.

Originally, every single culture across the globe honored the Mother Earth and women as the childbearers and many, many of these cultures honored the four directions. Very interesting similarities appeared throughout the planet in ancient times. All of the figurines that were made globally from ten thousand years ago and back before that were of the goddess. Now, can we get there from here? With modern technology having done what it's done, I'm not sure it will ever be the way it used to be. There was an old Earth First! slogan, "Back to the Pleistocene Era," and Judi Bari used to counter it by saying, "Onward to Ecotopia."

We have been given all of these incredible gifts. The gift of not having to die in childbirth. The gifts of modern medicine. All kinds of creature comforts that we have. We have taken these gifts and we have abused them. We have hoarded them. We have turned them into waste products instead of honoring them. To paraphrase what Einstein once said, the challenge of human beings is for our spiritual evolution to keep up with our technological evolution.

If you go back not a hundred years ago or so, people made their own clothing, made their own food, harvested their own wheat, and built their own houses. People take a lot better care of things they make than things they are just given in exchange for money. We need to get back in touch with the actual planet itself, the substances that it consists of, and back in touch with all of the cleverness we have and the understanding we need to honor the Earth instead of destroy it.

JM: I sense that a lot of people feel that they need to choose between social change and spiritual growth. They feel that they need to work either on themselves or work on the world. Tell me how you manage to do both things and how they are connected.

DC: You mentioned Gandhi earlier and he is perhaps the paragon of personal transformation as political transformation. Martin Luther King, Jr. is another fantastic example of this. And yet, how many activists out there, when they are planning their action, ask themselves, "What would Gandhi do?" or "What would Dr. King do?" We honor these people in the abstract, without trying to really understand what it was they were doing. Personal transformation and political change go hand in hand, they are completely interlinked. The naturalist, John Muir, once said if you tug on one thing, you will find it is connected to everything else.

There are people who are politically active who don't think they have to work on themselves personally or spiritually because they are doing good work in the world. And on the other side, there are people who are into yoga and meditation and feel that prayer alone or meditation alone is going to change the planet. Maybe we need to take that prayer to the Pentagon or take that prayer to the Federal Building.

Thinking that I can only be a spiritual person or I can only be an activist falls into the trap of getting into specialization. Because with specialization you have the doctor and the janitor that cleans the office and the doctor is now paid one thousand dollars an hour and the janitor is paid eight bucks an hour. And how can the janitor possibly afford to go to the doctor?

The whole notion of specialization is really ingrained in us. If you are a doctor, you can be a brain surgeon or a podiatrist or a pediatrician, but you can't be everything. Or if you're a scientist, you're a physicist or a chemist. It wasn't that long ago that we were all generalists and if you go back to tribal society, yes, somebody may have been the better arrowhead maker and somebody was the better shaman, but everybody knew how to use herbs and everybody knew how to make arrows. In that way, we also appreciated what everybody did a little more then we do now, because we did it ourselves.

JM: I hear some activists say that they feel inspired to take action through anger about the injustice that they see around them. Yet, I hear people who base their work in compassion do something else with their anger besides let it propel them into action. I imagine that you have been angry over the years at injustices and maybe even at the injustice directed towards you, such as the car bombing in 1990. What do you do with anger?

DC: I would be lying to you if I didn't tell you that I had my moments of anger. I certainly do, and no shortage of them. But I don't think that my activism is rooted in anger. I think if anything, it is rooted in a sense of bewilderment that we live on such a beautiful planet with such an abundance of everything and we choose to destroy it rather then just revel in it. For me, my awakening came from this puzzlement. I was just ten years old when I started to realize that people were for some reason destroying the great gift of this planet.

Especially today, when I hear people justify war and slaughter, at first I can't understand why they are saying this. But my friend, Bob Martel, said, "Find the truth in what everybody says." Those are very wise words. So, I start to listen. And I realize that there are a lot of reasons people say the things that they say. They are not all just evil reasons. For example, we as Westerners have an institutional mentality. If you don't honor only one God, if you don't throw away your herbs or you visit doctors who use leeches to suck out your disease, if you don't go to school, if you don't fight the war that the government tells you to fight, then you are going to be tortured and killed. And your family is going to be tortured and killed. There is a real institutional memory of this that goes back even before the Inquisition, right back to times of ancient Egypt.

The other thing is that perhaps we don't need to convince people that they are wrong. Perhaps what we need to do is show people a better way. That is a much more invigorating and positive and enlivening way to engage in activism than shaking your finger at somebody and saying, "You're wrong." Because guess what? Half of this country loves the Republican Party and the other half loves the Democratic Party and there's a few of us who believe that the whole system should be thrown out, so we have to get real and understand that we are dealing with a nation that is pretty much into monotheism and into warfare. Even if people are against hoarding everything for themselves and fighting somebody else's war, they don't necessarily know the way out.

I see music as one of the methods of enlightening people and perhaps breaking through that barrier between us that has been erected so high and for so long. Music has long been called the universal language. It is a way for everybody to get together and have a good time and sing, dance, and clap and get the truth out at the same time. When you do that with people who perhaps have a different political opinion then yours, it is harder to go to war with that person the next day. Judi Bari used to organize loggers and build bridges with the timber industry. She would say, "If you want somebody to see and understand your issue, if you want somebody to work on your issue, the first thing that you have to do is to work on theirs."

So many people are worried about their unemployment benefits or their medical insurance or the schooling that they have to go through or the safety of their neighborhood. Yet, activists tend to be very specialized and not reach out to these people. We have to resonate with the world community if we are going to bring ourselves away from the collision course we are on.

JM: Marshall Rosenberg, who writes about nonviolent communication, teaches that we can either try to be right and prove other people wrong or we can try to have connection with people. We can meet our needs and meet other people's needs at the same time. In politics, often there is this idea that the best we can do is compromise, which usually seems to mean that nobody gets their needs met. I notice that the second principle of Earth First! is "No compromise in the defense of Mother Earth." I wonder what the idea of compromise means to you.

DC: Well, the Earth is not ours to compromise. Who gives the Sierra Club lobbyists the right to sell out half of the forest? Who gives anybody the right to sell off ten percent of the ozone layer? It is not the right of human beings to be able to give these things away.

Should we have compromised with South Africa on apartheid? Should we have compromised with Hitler on the Holocaust? There are some things that you cannot compromise. You cannot compromise your integrity. Because once you compromise your integrity and the positions that follow with your integrity, you are on a slippery slope to corruption. Compromise is ultimately about corruption of the soul as well as corruption of politics.

What we are really talking about is finding common ground and finding the highest instead of the lowest common denominator. Some years ago, I went up to Ohio to work with United Steel workers who were on strike, but one of the steel workers there was fighting to save a single tree on his land. The county wanted to condemn his tree, which was a five-hundred-year-old oak, and cut it down to expand a remote county road by five or ten feet. The steel worker's family was fundamentalist Christian and worked in a very polluting industry. Their two sons were on the football team and they prayed to the Lord before dinner, but they wanted to save that tree. And they welcomed me—an Earth First! pagan—into their house, with open arms. And we all worked together to save their beloved oak. We started a letter writing campaign to the District Attorney and to the county and we saved the tree! These are people who, on the surface, I would have described as immensely different from myself. And yet we all came together around the tree; perhaps it was the tree of life, if you will.

**JM**: On June 11, 2002, you received a positive verdict in your and Judi Bari's case against the FBI and the Oakland Police Department. Tell us about that and also what the results have been of the Congressional Inquiry you initiated.

**DC**: There were a number of Congressional Inquiries into the bombing of Judi Bari and myself and also larger Congressional and Senatorial Inquiries into the FBI in general. All of those inquiries were abandoned after the September 11, 2001 attacks on the World Trader Center and the Pentagon. The 9/11 Commission then condemned the FBI as a complete failure. We need to take a real hard look at how absolutely inept and incompetent, as well as how vindictive and wrong-headed the FBI is.

Even though Judi Bari survived the car bombing, she died in 1997 from breast cancer, leaving myself and her estate, along with our fine legal team, to carry on our case against the FBI and Oakland Police Department. And it took us basically twelve years after the bombing to get our lawsuit to a courtroom in front of a jury. Perseverance is really essential if we are going to succeed at anything in this world. We can't fall prey to that whole fast food mentality. You may not eat at McDonald's or Taco Bell, but boycotting the mentality of the instant satisfaction, is more important than boycotting the actual restaurants themselves.

We stuck it out, and I can only tell you that sticking it out was a Herculean mission. It just took every ounce of our strength to pull it off. When we got to trial, a number of very magical things happened. We wound up with a jury that was eighty percent women. We had to be unanimous in the verdict and as soon as I saw that we had eighty percent women on the jury, I had that good feeling inside of me, because Judi Bari was the mother of two children and resonated very strongly with other women. I took that as a very good sign.

The FBI and the Oakland Police Department said they were totally justified in blaming Judi Bari and myself for bombing ourselves. They tried to say that we were terrorists and we advocated sabotage. I was questioned under oath about my album cover for *They Sure Don't Make Hippies Like They Used To*. It had cartoon representations of Judi Bari and myself walking away from a burning bulldozer with a monkey wrench in one hand and a can of gasoline in the other. I said, "That is a work of art. It is a political statement and that is not an actual bulldozer burning."

We were never charged with a crime. We were just accused of it and put in jail and then we were released without charges. When the jury came back with its verdict, they found the six officers guilty—of libel is the technical term—of violating our civil rights. The officers were found guilty of violating our First Amendment right to freedom of speech, and violating our Fourth Amendment right to protection from false arrest and illegal search and seizure.

It was so redeeming. The weight of the world had been lifted from our shoulders. And we won not for ourselves, but we won for everybody in this country and hopefully for everybody in the world.

**JM**: On *Real American*, there is a song called "The Ghosts of Mississippi." It is partly about the bombing. Tell me a little more about the making of music. What role does music play in your life now and in your activism?

**DC**: I come from a musical family. My grandfather played every instrument that there was and all of my uncles and cousins played instruments. I think it's in my blood. I started writing political songs when I was ten years old in 1966. They were about pollution and about the Vietnam war. They weren't necessarily very good songs, but from then on I saw myself as a topical songwriter.

If you are hanging out with a group of people around the campfire and you can make up a song about everybody hanging around the campfire and the work that they've done, people appreciate it. For me, the joy of making music is not having a top forty song on the radio, but inspiring the people who are immediately around me and the people who are working on the issues that I am singing about. If those songs could somehow or other find their way into radio stations, then so much the better.

I used to work for the music industry. In the seventies I worked for United Artist Records, at a smaller disco company called Roadshow Records. When I started working there, I really wanted to get a record contract and be a famous singer-songwriter. But from my corporate music experience in the seventies, I learned at the ripe old age of twenty-two that I never wanted to sign a record contract. I saw the way the music industry operated and I knew immediately I wanted no part of it.

For me, music is cellular. Everything in the universe and beyond vibrates. And everything that vibrates is making a sound. I call those sounds "song." Whether you're a star or you're an atom or a bird or a worm, or an asteroid whizzing through space, you've got a song to sing. That is why I think singing is so essential for turning humanity around into a place of appreciation for this planet. Every cell in our body is humming along to some tune.

# Darryl Cherney Selected Discography

*I Had To Be Born This Century* – 1987 (Churn It Up Records)
*They Sure Don't Make Hippies Like They Used To* – 1989 (Churn It Up Records)
*Timber!* with Judi Bari and George Shool – 1991 (Churn It Up Records)
*Who Bombed Judi Bari?* Spoken Word Album – 1997 (Alternative Tentacles)
*White Tribal Music* – 1999 (Churn It Up Records)
*Real American* – 2004 (Churn It Up Records)

# SAY LITTLE AND DO MUCH

## An Interview with Steve Reich

You are wherever your thoughts are.
—from *You Are (Variations)* by Steve Reich


STEVE REICH was born in New York in 1936 and grew up there and in California, traveling between the two by train to visit his separated parents. He began playing the drums at the age of fourteen, and became interested in the rhythmic aspects of music. He graduated with honors in philosophy from Cornell University and then studied composition with Hall Overton. From 1958 to 1961 he studied at the Juilliard School of Music with William Bergsma and Vincent Persichetti. Reich received his M.A. in music from Mills College in 1963, where he studied with Darius Milhaud and Luciano Berio, who encouraged his innovative approach to composition.

As a young student of musical composition, he sought out the indigenous music of Africa and Bali. These non-Western traditions contributed the elements of his favored compositional tools: non-traditional harmonic progressions, a conscious limitation of the number of musical elements, the pulsation of African and Balinese music, and phasing—the cyclical repetition of an audio clip or musical phrase, with the cycles slightly out of phase with each other. Reich, recently called "the most original musical thinker of our time" by the *New Yorker,* brought a type of "world music" to the West long before music stores and record companies began using this label.

Early in his career, in pieces such as *It's Gonna Rain* (1965) and *Come Out* (1966), Reich used speech recordings as a basis for his work. In 1988, he developed the method into a fuller "documentary music" style with his composition *Different Trains.* The music for this piece was based on interviews that were taped and then edited, a style that Reich used again in two high-tech music theater opera pieces created in collaboration with video artist Beryl Korot. *The Cave* (1990–93), represents an exploration of Biblical stories and *Three Tales* (2002) looks at the impact of technology on the world through three events: the crash of the German Hindenburg zeppelin in New Jersey in 1937 as Nazism was gaining momentum in Europe, the United States's atom bomb tests on the Bikini atoll from 1946 to 1954, and the cloning of Dolly the sheep in 1997.

The music of Steve Reich is unclassifiable: mesmerizing, original, engrossing, complex, eerie, and beautiful. The repetitive cycles, the pulsing and interlocking rhythms, the gentle shifting of melodic patterns, and the expansive textures all draw the listener in and awaken the senses. The music is full, but with room to breathe.

When I saw Reich perform *Music for Eighteen Musicians* and one section from *Three Tales* at San Francisco's Davies Symphony Hall in 2001, I felt I was seeing a divine ritual. A number of times during *Music for Eighteen Musicians*, one of the musicians would walk over and, with utmost clarity and concentration, take over the part of another musician playing marimbas or percussion without missing a beat. There was a sense of community within the shifting human forms.

The social and spiritual themes of some of his compositions, such as *Three Tales* and *Tehillim*, explore cultural attitudes while offering insights into the mysteries of life and death. Reich conveys a deep curiosity about the place of humans in the universe, the relationship between our thoughts and actions, and the origin of the compassionate desire to contribute to the world.

Jewish spirituality and religious texts are components of many of Reich's works, from the Hebrew Psalms of *Tehillim*:

> Keep your tongue from evil
> and do good
> Seek peace
> and pursue it

to *The Cave*, based on interviews with Israelis, Palestinians, and Americans concerning the relationships between Abraham, Sarah, Hagar, Ishmael, and Isaac in the Old Testament. His own life as a Jew informs other pieces: his 1988 composition *Different Trains* looks at the period between 1939 and 1941 when he was traveling across the United States and Jewish children his age in Europe were traveling on other trains.

Reich's willingness to let go of the rigid structures of classical serialism has led him to rich musical discoveries. He based the 1981 *Tehillim* on Hebrew phrases and syllables, arranging the music according to his interpretation of the rhythm of the Hebrew language. The piece diverges from the traditional grouping of notes into small uniform measures and instead articulates musical phrases in groups of twos and threes in totally free arrangement, as well as in groups of very large measures. Reich has since utilized the resulting patterns in many other works.

Steve Reich's compositions have been performed worldwide by major orchestras and ensembles and choreographed for dancers by Anna Theresa de Keersmaeker, Jiri Kylian, Jerome Robbins, Laura Dean, Alvin Ailey, and Lucinda Childs. A tribute album, *Reich Remixed*, released in 1999, features remixes of Reich's compositions by DJs such as Coldcut, Howie B, and DJ Spooky. His latest composition, *You Are (Variations)*, premiered in Los Angeles in October 2004, and in Germany and London in January 2005.

*You Are (Variations)* brings together Reich's recognizable rhythm-based music, emphasizing human voice and percussion, with a continued exploration of the human experience. The piece is based on four main phrases: "You are wherever your thoughts are," from eighteenth century Hassidic rabbi Nachman of Breslov; "I place the eternal before me" from the Psalms; "Explanations come to an end somewhere," by philosopher Ludwig Wittgenstein; and from Pirkei Avot, one of the oldest parts of the Talmud, "Say little and do much."

▼ ▼ ▼ ▼ ▼

**John Malkin**: In 1965, you produced a piece called *It's Gonna Rain* that dealt with the human potential to destroy the world. Later you composed *Different Trains*, which deals with the Holocaust. In the section of *Three Tales* titled "Dolly," we hear an interviewee say, "The twentieth century is the worst graveyard in human history." I sense that your compositions, particularly the documentary sound compositions, are filled with both the joy of life and also compassion for those who are suffering. What is the underlying intention and philosophy of your compositions?

**Steve Reich**: I don't have any underlying philosophy for anything I do. I am a religious person practicing traditional Judaism. I am not a philosophical one, although I studied philosophy. If you study Ludwig Wittgenstein, he said, "Get an honest job." By which he meant, "Go out and do something real in the world and don't teach philosophy." So I followed his advice.

I take each piece as it comes. In purely musical pieces, the problems are musical. In *It's Gonna Rain*, I was balancing the voice and the melodic character of that voice, coupled with the meaning, which was preaching about Noah and the flood and basically the end of the world. In 1962, I was in San Francisco during the Cuban missile crisis and it felt like we could all go up in so much radioactive smoke. So, in 1965, this preacher really laying it down about Noah and the flood and the end of the world had a lot of resonance with what was going on. It is a piece about the end of the world, and the cloud is still over us.

There is no underlying grand vision. Each piece presents its own problems that have to be figured out. Of course, one piece will influence another and I guess I have recurring interests that pop up. Sometimes I am surprised to see them.

JM: I do sense an ongoing religious exploration in your music. Where does that come from?

SR: I think one day they're going to put electrodes on us and find out that some people are genetically disposed to ritual and religious practice. My mother has that. My father did not. I was raised a reform Jew, which means I learned basically nothing—no Hebrew, I didn't know the Torah was read in an annual cycle, I didn't understand anything about the holidays. I didn't know who Rashi—the great medieval Biblical commentator—was.

I became involved in the early sixties with Hatha yoga and *pranayama*, the breathing exercises that go with it. Later, I discovered some Buddhist meditation exercises and Transcendental Meditation, as everybody was involved with it in those days. It did me a lot of good. It was very focusing, very calming.

But around 1974, I began to feel that something was missing. And I suddenly got the thought that maybe I could find it in my own backyard. But I'd have to, so to speak, go in and dig up the crabgrass and get some new information. I ended up doing an adult study at Lincoln Square Synagogue, a traditional Orthodox synagogue in New York, where they had a very good adult education program. I learned some Biblical Hebrew. I began studying Torah and the commentaries. And I began changing my life through religious practice. I began to avoid giving concerts on Friday nights and to observe the Sabbath. My practice has been growing apace ever since.

JM: It seems that your religious practice translates into a desire to present to the world some food for thought, challenging violent and destructive relationships between human beings. A lot of people seem to feel a need to choose between being religious or being involved in social change.

SR: I don't think that's a choice. I think the two go together very easily. Religion, in Judaism certainly, requires a lot of things to be done. Faith is essential to Judaism, but *doing* is what matters. And doing precedes everything else. When you do, you change in the process of doing. Your faith and your understanding and everything else grow from those actions, whether you are limiting your diet, limiting your sexual activities, changing your schedule, or observing sundown Friday to sundown Saturday as a period of cessation. These things will tend to change your outlook on life. So the actions come first.

JM: One of the interviewees in *Three Tales* says, "It is terrible to think of the spiritual impulse as arising from cognitive weakness."

SR: Right. In other words, "Religious people aren't stupid." There is a presumption, particularly in the West, that anyone who is religious, which translates into being Christian, is a numbskull. That's a foolish characterization. I think a lot of very, very intelligent, very well-informed people are religious people who are not dangerous fundamentalists. These intelligent religious people are sort of swept under the rug by those who would characterize religion as a lack of cognitive ability. Marx's idea that "Religion is the opiate of the masses" is a worn-out cliché. Give me a break.

JM: In *Three Tales*, someone says, "To some extent, evolution has become its own religion." In other words, maybe science has taken on qualities of religion.

SR: Let's put it this way—I think everybody is religious. What do I mean by that? I mean whatever it is that for you defines ultimate reality—your barometer of the real truth of a matter—*that* is your religion. Now, a lot of people, without thinking about it, just accept scientific explanations of things as the true and complete story. Anything else is superstition, old wives' tales, what have you. And when that scientific view is even questioned as the sole explanation of everything that goes on in the universe, people often take offense, which is truly, unbeknownst to them, an offense to their *religion*.

JM: There are three subjects in *Three Tales*: the destruction of the Hindenburg aircraft, the atomic bomb tests in the Bikini Islands by the U.S. government, and the cloning of Dolly the sheep. What connects them?

SR: It isn't completely spelled out, but basically we were trying to present technology in the twentieth century—early, middle, and late. We chose the crash of the Hindenburg in 1937 because it was the first time something like that was caught on film. When the *Titanic* went down, there was nobody around with a camera. With the Hindenburg, cameras were grinding away and all of a sudden this group of dignitaries crossing the Atlantic literally went up in flames.

We chose Bikini because the atomic bomb is the emblematic technology of the twentieth century, and Hiroshima and Nagasaki have been so well-documented that we thought we'd avoid them. "Bikini" highlights the interface between what was *the* highest technology on the planet and these people on the Bikini Islands who are about as far from technology as any human beings on Earth could be. This megalith forced them off of their island, and to this day they have not been able to go back.

We didn't know what the third act was going to be, but when Dolly was cloned while we were working on "Hindenburg" and "Bikini," Beryl Korot, the video artist, and I just looked at each other and said, "That's it!" Because cloning was obviously the beginning of a whole new chapter in biology and medicine, taking technology, as Beryl points out, *into* our bodies. Not building machines outside, but actually beginning to put things, whether genes or implants, into the human body—this is already in the early stages and will play out in the twenty-first century.

The thread is a little bit pointed out by the biblical underpinnings, as a retelling of the stories of Genesis. In Genesis there are two stories of the creation of man. The first one is probably better known than the second. The first is where man is given dominion over all the birds of the air, the fish of the sea, and everything that moves upon the face of the Earth. And indeed we do have that dominion. African Pygmies could bring down an elephant with a blowgun thousands of years ago. Whether we like it or not, we have that power and we have the responsibility that goes with having that power.

On the other hand, there is a second story of creation. The second story of creation is that Ha Adam, the human being—not the man, the human being—is made from a lump of dirt and Hashem the Eternal blows directly into his nostrils the breath of life and places the being—which then turns into both a man and a woman—in the garden. It says in Hebrew, *l'avdah v' l'shomra*, to serve it and to keep it. Now, that's a very different set of marching orders. That's to maintain it and keep it in good working order because if you mess it up, there's no one else to clean up the mess.

So we have this tension between the fact that we have enormous amounts of power, which we really do have, and which we really should use. But the question is, How? And that is the thread, if you like, underlying all of these pieces. What it shows is that as time passes, the chips mount up. The stakes are higher and the risks are greater.

**JM:** I find *Three Tales* to be really chilling, especially the third section on cloning and robotics. Some of the people interviewed for the composition point to the human possibility of living without death, as well as the ability to *create* life.

**SR:** We are presenting people like Marvin Minsky, who is the father of artificial intelligence up at MIT, and Rodney Brooks, who is the head of robotics at MIT, and Richard Dawkins, the biologist at Oxford, and James Watson, who discovered DNA, and lots of other people. Rabbi Adin Steinsaltz, who studied science as a young man and became one of the foremost rabbis of our time, has a different take on things. There are lots of other scientists with very different views and outlooks. Steven Pinker, the psychologist, is briefly in the piece and, of course, he has a very different outlook from Richard Dawkins. And Rodney Brooks has a very different outlook from, let's say, James Watson.

Ray Kurzweil is an interesting guy. He's the one who invented the Kurz-weil keyboard as a result of meeting Stevie Wonder. He invented a reading machine for the blind, so he has done a lot of interesting and wonderful things. He has also written a book called *The Age of Spiritual Machines*, in which he suggests that you or I, our thoughts and our conscious activity, could sup-posedly—and again a lot of people raise their eyebrows on just simply the reality factor here—be taken as electrical impulses and downloaded onto a disk, transferred into a robot, and *you* will live forever. Now, feel a whole lot better?

**JM**: These people are talking about the potential for creating a species that will be smarter than human beings and will displace humans.

**SR**: It is chilling to hear the dispassionate delivery that sometimes goes with that idea for some people. Other people, like Bill Joy, are very concerned with the idea you brought up. He is the chief scientist at Sun Microsystems and he did the lion's share of the work on inventing Java, without which we would have no internet. He's not just some guy out there who is living in a teepee and doesn't like technology—he's really in the thick of it. He is work-ing on a book right now that extends an article he wrote for *Wired* magazine a couple of years back called "Why the Future Doesn't Need Us," "us" being the human race. He's genuinely concerned and feels that it is the human responsibility of scientists to look into the implications of what they are doing *before* they do it. Again, as I say, the scientists interviewed in *Dolly* have very different views and responses to the possibility of eliminating the human race.

**JM**: You have said that contrary to the view that some people have of your music as being hypnotic or trance-inducing—especially your earlier music—that you have wanted people "to be wide awake and hear details they've never heard before." In the liner notes from *The Desert Music*, from 1983, you say in an interview, "One has to be in relative stillness to hear things in detail." I wonder what role that stillness plays in your life now and in your compos-ing, and what your feelings are about the contemporary quickening of life's tempo, leaving less and less stillness and quiet?

**SR**: I am talking to you from New York City and it's noisy here. I never walk out on the street here without my earplugs, which I keep in my pocket at all times. And that's not a nice way to live. So I spend as much time as I can in Vermont, where, when I take a walk outside, the loudest sound is my own footsteps. I live in the Green Mountain National Forest, so we are really about as far away from the lifestyle and noise level of New York City as it's possible to be in the eastern United States.

There is no easy answer to how to have stillness. People are free to live in cities or outside of cities, but it is economically harder to live outside of cities. A lot of people come to cities simply so they can find employment. It changes their lifestyle and it gathers them into a more high-tech, more high-pressure style of life. I am just a composer, not a sociologist or a social worker. But I am a human being and I think a lot of people are trying to find ways of either living outside of cities or spending some time outside of cities to put the brakes on one way or another.

JM: I enjoy the rhythm and texture and the pulsing of your music, as well as the way you craft text and the placement of words. I am particularly moved when there is a religious or spiritual component juxtaposed with other points of view. In *Three Tales*, for example, in the midst of this discussion about creating life and creating a robotic species, we hear someone say, "Every creature has a song."

SR: That is Rabbi Adin Steinsaltz: "The song of the fox, the song of the dog, the song of the fly, what do they say?" And then we cut to Ray Kurzweil who says, "Technology is a continuation of evolution." Rabbi Adin Steinsaltz is aware of all those realities, but he looks at Darwin as an explanation of, in a sense, how G-d can be seen as creating the world. There had to have been some actual way that happened and science brings that to light. Appreciating that doesn't demand a lessening of religious faith. It is simply an insight into a small, tiny part of how G-d works. Science explains some of the methodology of creation and the sustaining of creation.

JM: Where does the pulse come from that drives a lot of the music you've made?

SR: Well, I was a drummer when I was fourteen. I guess you could say that indicated a genetic disposition I was born with. G-d knows. I was a drummer and I admired Miles Davis and later spent a lot of time listening to John Coltrane and his drummer Elvin Jones. And I became interested in West African drumming through reading a book called *Studies in African Music* by A.M. Jones. I ended up going to Ghana in the summer of 1970 to study the drumming of the Ewe tribe, with members of the Ewe tribe and some Ashantis as well. I got malaria when I was in West Africa and I decided, "No more tropical trips for me," so I studied Balinese music in northern California at the American Society for Eastern Arts in the early 1970s. I worked with Balinese teachers and also formed a group of my own.

I was looking for musical traditions around the world where percussion was the main voice of the orchestra. The gamelan, which is the orchestra in Indonesia—and I am thinking of Bali in particular—is made up of metallaphones. Sort of similar to the Western vibraphone, only without the motor, and smaller and tuned differently and all different sizes and shapes of these slabs of metal over resonators. And there is perhaps one stringed instrument and one voice, but just as the symphony orchestra has an overwhelming number of strings, the gamelan has an overwhelming number of percussion instruments.

Similarly, in West Africa, drums, rattles, and bells are the main instruments. People will sing, of course, and there will be other instruments occasionally, but drums are primary. Those cultures produced a body of what we would call classical music. However, since the line between what is classical music and what is folk music is blurred and they all swing and they're all intentionally rhythmic, it becomes a question of which music is used for which occasions. They all share a certain very marked rhythmic pulse.

I was drawn to those kinds of music. And my music has always had that rhythmic vitality. I will be sixty-eight in October and thank G-d it's still going. If I make it to 2006, I will be seventy. There will be something going on in southern California, at Lincoln Center, at Brooklyn Academy of Music, at Carnegie Hall here in New York, at the Barbican Centre in London, and in Paris, Germany, and elsewhere.

JM: I have the impression that after you do a big project with video and text, you like to then do something that is purely music.

SR: Yes. I need a pit stop, like a racing driver. And this pit stop could be a good long one because when you work with musical ideas—purely musical ideas—you get fueled. And then if you do a music/theater piece, you've got some new harmonic ideas, new melodic ideas, new ways of working, that work themselves into that. So for the next few years I will be working on purely musical pieces.

The piece after this is going to be for the London Sinfonietta and for the dancer Akram Khan, who was a student of Anna Theresa de Keersmaeker, a choreographer whose work I think is probably the best choreography ever done to my music. She has choreographed *Music for Eighteen Musicians* and *Drumming* and a few other pieces. One of her students is also trained in Indian classical dancing, so I am writing a piece for him that will be for three string quartets and two pianos and four percussion. And then after that I am going to write a piece for my own ensemble. All of that will be presented in 2006.

JM: Do you think we'll ever hear any more phasing type of music?

SR: I stopped doing the phasing procedure in 1972, after *Drumming*. I haven't done it since. It is an idiosyncratic technique and I thought, Basta! I'd done a lot of it. And I don't see the need for it anymore. You know, *Music for Eighteen Musicians* doesn't use any phasing and a lot of the earlier pieces don't use it either. So I think that technique is one that I have hung up and left to dry out and if anybody else wants to use it, they can be my guest.

JM: Well, I might try it out!

SR: [Laughter] Okay! It's yours!

# Steve Reich Selected Discography

*Live Electronic Music: It's Gonna Rain; Violin Phase* – 1969 (Columbia Records)

*Come Out* – 1970 (Odyssey)

*Four Organs; Phase Patterns* – 1971 (Shandar)

*Drumming/Six Pianos/Music For Mallet Instruments* – 1974 (Deutsche Grammophon)

*Music For Eighteen Musicians* – 1978/1999/2004 (ECM/RCA/Amalinda)

*Variations For Winds, Strings And Keyboards* – 1979 (Philips)

*Octet; Music For Large Ensemble; Violin Phase* – 1980 (ECM)

*Tehillim* – 1982/1995/2002 (ECM/Nonesuch Records/Cantaloupe)

*Desert Music* – 1985 (Nonesuch Records)

*Sextet* – 1986 (Nonesuch Records)

*Different Trains; Electric Counterpoint* – 1989 (NonesuchRecords)

*The Four Sections; Music For Mallet...* – 1990 (Nonesuch Records)

*City Life* – 1995 (Nonesuch Records)

*The Cave* – 1995 (Nonesuch Records)

*Works: 1965-1995* – 1997 (Nonesuch Records)

*New York Counterpoint; Four Organs; Eight Lines* – 2000 (Nonesuch Records)

*Triple Quartet; Music For Large Ensemble* – 2001 (Nonesuch Records)

*Variations; Six Pianos* – 2002 (Deutsche Grammophon)

*Early Works: Clapping Music; Come Out; It's Gonna Rain; Piano Phase* – 2002 (Nonesuch Records)

*Eight Lines; City Life; New York Counterpoint; Violin Phase* – 2003 (RCA Records)

*Three Tales* – 2003 (Nonesuch Records)

# THE SOULS ARE COMING BACK

## AN INTERVIEW WITH HOLLY NEAR

Once upon a time there was a power,
so great that no one could know its name.
People tried to claim it and rule with it.
Always such arrogance ended in shame.
Thousands of years would pass in a moment.
Hundreds of cultures would come and go.
Each generation with a glorious calling,
even when they were too busy to know.
Then one day after two millennia,
which, after all, was a small part of time,
hundreds of souls found their way out of nowhere
to be on Earth at the threat of decline.
—from "Planet Called Home" by Holly Near

IT WAS A BRIGHT AND SUNNY DAY when I met Holly Near at the 13th annual Bioneers Conference, one of the largest annual gatherings of activists, teachers, and artists from around the world. In the afternoon, I sat down to interview Near following a panel discussion on "Art and Social Change" that had included herself; John Densmore, drummer for the legendary rock band the Doors; and film producer and marketing consultant Paula Silver.

Earlier that day, Tom Hayden, a longtime Civil Rights activist, author, and former California state senator, introduced Holly Near to a vibrant audience as an old friend and "one of the great voices of this movement in the world."

On stage and in person, Holly Near exudes a sense of optimism and integrity. Her work is a reminder that we can continually express and cultivate our intentions and actions for peace, freedom, and justice. Her work is a testament to the idea that we can manifest compassion in ourselves and in the world.

"We need our creativity now more then ever," she told the gathered Bioneers, as she broke into a rousing a cappella version of the song "Planet Called Home" from her 2000 album *Edge*. The words and energy of this spirited song set an invigorating and gracious tone for the day:

> Fabulous creatures sent from the power,
> souls that have come with one purpose in mind,
> to do one thing that will alter the outcome
> and maybe together we'll do it in time.

With thousands of us clapping to the beat, the song came to an end with a line repeated three times, slowing and quieting:

> The Souls are coming back,
> the Souls are coming back,
> the Souls are coming back.

She motioned to the audience of activists, now on their feet and clapping, and declared, "That would be you!"

Holly Near was born in Ukiah, California and raised by parents who were political activists and ranchers. She began singing publicly when she was eight years old and began her professional career with performances in films and television shows, including *Slaughterhouse Five* and *The Partridge Family*. Over the years, Near has collaborated with a variety of artists including Pete Seeger, Ronnie Gilbert, Arlo Guthrie, Mercedes Sosa, Bernice Johnson Reagon, Bonnie Raitt, and Cris Williamson.

In 1972, Holly Near founded Redwood Records, the first independent record company in the United States created by a woman. For twenty years the company recorded and promoted politically conscious artists from around the world, including musicians from Nicaragua, Chile, Australia, Canada, England, Argentina, Cuba, Uruguay, Vietnam, El Salvador, Mexico, and the United States. Calico Tracks Music is the independent label that she created to produce and distribute her most recent albums.

Twenty-five years ago, Near was one of the first openly lesbian singers. In concerts, she would lead large crowds in choruses of, "We are gay and straight together, singing for our lives," from her song "Singing for Our Lives," which she wrote after the murders of San Francisco city supervisor Harvey Milk and San Francisco mayor George Moscone.

Near has participated in the massive protests against the war in Vietnam, the U.S. military interventions and covert operations in Nicaragua, El Salvador, and Chile, the apartheid regime in South Africa, and the current war in Iraq. Near has received awards from the ACLU, the National Lawyers Guild, the National Organization for Women, and was named "woman of the year" by *Ms.* magazine in 1985.

Holly Near strives to create the world that she would like to live in, where bombs are no longer dropped and the sounds of music and freedom prevail. Her commitment to art and activism reminds us that there is no time to waste in releasing our own fear and anger and cultivating compassionate action for social change. "Notice the speed at which the Civil Rights movement transformed the world," she writes. "It did not fix the world, it transformed it. By noticing, by giving weight to participation, the next social change movement makes its way through chaos and prepares a surprise attack on our sleeping leadership. My faith is continually renewed."

▼ ▼ ▼ ▼ ▼

**John Malkin:** You've spoken about how you find courage in seeing courage displayed by others. Tell me about that and its connection to your music.

**Holly Near:** I like the idea of seeing one's life as part of a journey. I learned from Dr. Bernice Johnson Reagon, the founder of Sweet Honey in the Rock and one of the original freedom singers in the Civil Rights movement, you don't start from scratch; there is always something that came before. If you're on a path, it inherently means that someone walked there before you, otherwise it would just be overgrown. And paths change, turning in one direction and another.

There are very few moments when you're actually the first person starting something from scratch. We all walk in the splendor and the horror of that which has gone before us. This gives me a context in which to be alive on the planet. Without this context, being in the world would be just too lonely. A life would be like a note that was just sort of off dangling somewhere.

I just heard that Ysaye Barnwell, also of Sweet Honey in the Rock, does a singing workshop where she first teaches all of the harmonies and then puts the melody in last, instead of the other way around. The moment that melody enters, all of the people who have been singing the harmony go, "Ahhh." It lifts them, because they didn't know where it was going. Notes by themselves are not nearly as interesting to me as when they come into relationship with others.

And I feel that about work and about people, it is the relationship that matters. I'm not always good at how I do relationships. But life is an opportunity to practice.

JM: How do you see social change and spirituality being connected? Sometimes in the progressive or radical change movements in the United States, spirituality is thrown out along with religion, which is thought of as an "opiate for the masses." Do you see them supporting each other towards positive change?

HN: We're not static creatures, so we go through phases where our perspectives change. Your perspective on the role of religion and spirituality also has a lot to do with your background. Some people who came from northern European descent have felt a great deal of pain and agony over the fact that people of that culture committed great genocide in the name of God. They remember how the Church had controlled women's bodies and burned women at the stake. Great violence had taken place under the name of religion and many political thinkers who followed felt that religion had kept people down.

There were parts of the Bible that were pulled out or deliberately misinterpreted. The Bible says, "The meek shall inherit the Earth." But that was interpreted to mean, "After they die, they'll inherit it in heaven; right now the rich people are going to get it!" New theology came along in Central and Latin America, people who had come through Catholicism told a different Biblical story. They said, "The meek shall inherit the Earth *now*. We're not waiting until we die and go to heaven. We are going to begin creating quality of life for us on Earth. Heaven is here on Earth."

Then there are women who are coming to spiritual practice by looking back to ancient matriarchal religions. Native Americans have a whole spirituality in relationship to nature and the drum and ritual. And you have the African American communities, particularly in the South, for whom the Christian church has been a major organizing center. So these people's whole relationship to God and religion is really different than those people who have felt oppressed by religion. This spirituality was their revolutionary lifeline. So people come to religions through very different doors.

There are actually so many things in my life that are turning out better than I imagined them. Early feminism is one example. If someone had said to me, "This woman is going to come along and she is going to write this play called *The Vagina Monologues*. It's going to be a big hit," I would say, "No way! No way!" Well, not only did it happen, it is part of a movement all over the world to confront violence against women. It is very easy to get depressed and demoralized, but the fact is that extraordinary things are going on.

JM: You have been a witness to, and played a role in, social change for so long. What role does music and creativity play in social change?

HN: A song can educate, inform, support, give courage, inspire, or pacify. Music gets used in all those different ways. A marching band can send young people off to war. That same marching band at the Gay Pride Parade in San Francisco sends people off to love. You can have a lullaby that puts a child to sleep or you can have muzak that puts a whole nation to sleep. Music is a very powerful gift we have access to and people should take it seriously.

The music that led the marches in the Civil Rights movement gave people the courage to face Jim Crow. In the Civil Rights movement, the labor movement, the women's movement, and the gay liberation movement, people found songs that were saving their lives by letting them know they weren't alone.

Young people feel very frustrated when they don't get heard. Rock 'n' roll came along and our parents, except for some really radical, out-there parents, couldn't hear what young people were saying. It is really important that the older generation hears what the younger one is saying. But it also matters what musical format they are using to say it.

JM: It seems that it is in the nature of new language, such as hip hop, that it is misunderstood.

HN: Young people usually create the next language. When I was first starting in the women's movement, we didn't have a lot of the words we use today. Maybe those words existed in the dictionary, but we didn't use them. Words like "hate crimes" and "homophobia" weren't part of our language. Language comes up as necessary.

There is a film out now about Billie Holliday's song, "Strange Fruit." That song was one of the first to talk about lynching in a way that reached a larger audience. In a very essential way, it altered people's consciousness about lynching, and in such a melodic way. The song was written and sung for the general population almost in code. You did not know what that song was about unless you focused on the lyrics, "Strange fruit, hanging from a tree."

Now young people are coming out of poverty and coming out of abuse and using their own music to tell about it. Young people in prisons, in institutions, and in juvenile halls are being treated so badly. They are telling these stories and other young people are listening to them, but many of the people who are in positions of political power are not hearing these stories. I think it is important to figure out how they can get their voices heard. And that means being heard in many languages and being heard by young and old.

JM: I heard you tell two very powerful stories earlier today. Would you tell me those stories now?

HN: The first is of a man in Sarajevo who was a cellist, and went out into a town square while bombs were dropping and began to play his cello. Someone from the press walked up to him and said, "Sir, why are you out here playing your cello while they are dropping bombs?" And his response was, "Why are they dropping bombs when I am playing my cello?"

This is an example of how essential it is that we rephrase the questions. The media and the politicians have decided that they are the ones who are going to ask the questions. And the questions are usually asked in a very shallow and fact-free environment. By the way they ask the question, they will articulate the answer they want to hear. And in this way the cellist rephrased the question and opened it up to a huge, global perspective. Let's rethink our priorities. I love that story because in one brief moment you can articulate the essential need to open the question up to a bigger picture.

When I was in New York, I saw a father hit a child. The child was very young and was just not walking fast enough and got hit. I know that parents reach the end of their ropes. But those frustrations are not our children's. They don't belong to them. They are ours, and we have to find ways to work through them. I was going to try to do an intervention. We see violence in the grocery stores all of the time, whether it is emotional or physical. But it is very hard to intervene without embarrassing the parent who already feels so bad. They might just hit the kid even more if they feel shamed by their actions.

Across the street from us was a young black man with long dreadlocks and a very joyful energy. He saw the father hit the kid and he started dancing in the street and singing, "Don't hit the baby! Don't hit the baby." It was simple, nonviolent, and non-confrontational. So amazing! The father seemed able to hear it and was kind of stunned. It didn't provoke his violence. People around the street got to hear it. We all got informed.

This story tells me that we never know who is watching. But if we behave in little ways every day, if we act our truth in a totally loving way, we can alter the street corner. This was such a great example of participatory government. As a songwriter, as a human being, my goal continues to be to make change in the world in this peaceful, harmonious, and nonviolent way. That is in keeping with who I am. There are many different ways to be an activist. How a young person in Oakland responds may be different from how an elder in Palestine responds, which may be different from how a new mother in Kenya responds. I try to stay alert, to notice, to acknowledge, to learn. Nature and humanity are my teachers. For me, that is the most influential guide to activism.

# Holly Near Selected Discography

*Hang In There* – 1973 (Redwood Records)

*A Live Album* – 1975 (Redwood Records)

*You Can Know All I Am* – 1976 (Redwood Records)

*Imagine My Surprise* with Meg Christian – 1978 (Redwood Records)

*Fire In the Rain* – 1981 (Redwood Records)

*Speed of Light* – 1982 (Redwood Records)

*Journeys, A Retrospective: 1972-1983* – 1983 (Redwood Records)

*Lifeline* with Ronnie Gilbert – 1983/2002 (Redwood Records/Appleseed Recordings)

*Watch Out!* with John McCutcheon and Trapezoid – 1984 (Redwood Records)

*Sing To Me the Dream* with Inti Illimani – 1984 (Redwood Records)

*Harp* with Arlo Guthrie, Ronnie Gilbert, and Pete Seeger – 1985/2001 (Redwood Records/ Appleseed Recordings)

*Singing With You* with Ronnie Gilbert – 1987 (Redwood Records)

*Don't Hold Back* – 1987 (Redwood Records)

*Sky Dances* – 1989 (Redwood Records)

*Singer in the Storm* – 1990 (Chameleon Music Group)

*Musical Highlights from Fire in The Rain* – 1993 (Calico Tracks)

*This Train Still Runs* with Ronnie Gilbert – 1996 (Abbe Alice Music)

*With a Song in My Heart* with John Bucchino – 1997 (Calico Tracks Music)

*Simply Love: The Women's Music Collection* – 2000 (Calico Tracks Music)

*Edge* – 2000 (Calico Tracks Music)

*Early Warnings* – 2001 (Appleseed Recordings)

*And Still We Sing* – 2002 (Calico Tracks Music)

*Crushed* – 2002 (Calico Tracks Music)

*Cris & Holly* with Cris Williamson – 2003 (HC Records)

# CHANGE IT ALL

AN INTERVIEW WITH GOAPELE MOHLABANE

Sometimes you just have to let it go
Leaving all of my fears to burn down
Push them all away so I can move on
Closer to my dreams
—from "Closer" by Goapele

GOAPELE MOHLABANE was born in Oakland, California, in 1977 to a Jewish mother from New York and a South African father. Her name means "to go forward" in Tswana, the South African dialect of her grandmother. Her father, political exile Douglas Mohlabane, met her mother, Noa, in Nairobi, Kenya. Goapele grew up touched by the histories of both sides of her family: her father's family's great suffering during the apartheid regime in South Africa and the murder of her maternal great-grandparents by the Nazis. In Goapele's childhood home, art and activism were deeply linked. She grew up believing that music, theater, and dance are inseparable from struggles for justice and peace.

Goapele began making music as a young girl, performing for family and friends. When she was fourteen, she joined the Oakland Youth Chorus. Later, she became a member of the semiprofessional performance group, Vocal Motion. She studied at the Berklee College of Music in Boston and then returned to the Bay Area to collaborate with her brother Namane on his DJ and production project, Local 1200.

In 2001, Goapele released the ten-song EP *Closer,* which she produced and distributed with her family. It sold three thousand copies. Her reputation as a dynamic singer began to spread and she began performing regularly at clubs and concerts. In 2002, Goapele reworked *Closer,* adding five new songs, and released it with the new title, *Even Closer*. To distribute the new album, she formed the independent label Skyblaze Recordings with Theo Rodrigues and her brother Namane. *Even Closer* was nominated in 2003 for the California Music Award for Outstanding R&B album. And in 2003, *Rolling Stone* magazine described Goapele as one of its "Ten Artists to Watch" and as a singer who presents "…a balance of steamrolling Chaka Khan power and yoga-girl suppleness that's full of promise."

Her diverse influences, from Etta James, Nina Simone, Stevie Wonder, Billie Holiday, Bob Marley, Prince, and Portishead to Miriam Makeba and Hugh Masekela are reflected in both the style of her music and the content of her songs. *Even Closer* is an album based on her personal experiences and the lives of others, with songs about relationships, the struggles of those in her community, and the worldwide problems of violence and racism. She expresses her own dismay about the September 11, 2001, attacks on the World Trade Center, and the U.S. government's war response to the event, in the song "Red, White, and Blues." In this song and others on the album, Goapele has created soulful and beautiful music that speaks to the changes she wants to see in the world.

Goapele and I shared a cup of tea at her new recording studio in Emeryville, California. The building is being remodeled to serve her musical needs and there is a feeling of excitement among her family and colleagues about the positive changes around her. As the interview drew to a close, microphone stands and amps were being set up in an adjacent room for an evening rehearsal of material that will be recorded for her next album, tentatively titled *Change It All*.

▼ ▼ ▼ ▼ ▼

**John Malkin**: Congratulations on the success of your music and on distributing your music independently. I think that's an important thing to have done.

**Goapele Mohlabane**: It's been a continuously growing project. The music started before we'd even organized a label. Now Skyblaze is with Columbia and we are going to put out a new album soon.

JM: How did you come to start Skyblaze?

GM: It was really out of necessity. I had been into music for a long time. At Berklee, I wanted to write songs. I wasn't really taking songwriting classes, but studying a lot of theory and meeting different people. I started writing and soon ended up with a pretty good amount of songs. I realized I wanted to put out the album when I moved back to the Bay Area and started hooking up with other producers such as Amp Live, Johnson, and Mike Tiger from The Coup. When we had about ten songs that I felt pretty good about, my family helped me put out the album. I had the material that I wanted to get out into the world, but it didn't really fit a category and I didn't know how the industry was going to take it. I just wanted to see how people would react to my music.

So we figured out a way to get some money together, just enough to duplicate a couple thousand CDs. We were selling them at shows and some local retail stores. The album did pretty well there, so we decided to officially start a record label, keep recording, and rerelease the CD as *Even Closer*, officially under Skyblaze, and the distribution just grew from there.

JM: How do you bring ideas about social change into your music?

GM: I remember thinking about different issues when I was in kindergarten! I was really curious about race, mainly. Both sides of my family have been through some intense, crazy political situations. From the time I was young, my parents were very community-oriented and we always had a lot of people over. A lot of the music that we listened to was socially conscious music, whether it was Hugh Masekela or Miriam Makeba or Bob Marley, Stevie Wonder, or Nina Simone. And of course all of these artists are also singing love songs. There has always been that mixture. From early on, I could see how important it is to not be afraid to speak up. Maybe if there were more of us who had spoken up earlier, we might not be in this situation that we are in now. Whether it's through art or through music or organizing, it is important to speak up about what we believe is right.

As a teenager, I started singing at some underground hip hop events and different rallies. We were trying to make it so that youth didn't have a curfew in Oakland, when that was being proposed. We were trying to make the laws not so crazy for youth. Lately I have been in a live music scene, performing at a lot of concerts and clubs.

I try to integrate my politics into my own music and just say what I feel like saying. I just say my little pieces to my audiences, wherever I perform, even if it's not a political environment.

JM: So, at a show at a jazz club, would you say something about current political events?

GM: It really depends on what's happening. I like to take advantage of the opportunity to share my thoughts and music with a lot of people, regardless of where they're coming from. They might just be coming together for music, but I definitely see it as an opportunity and I really go with the vibe.

On the last album, I had this song called "Red, White, and Blues" that was just talking about 9/11. I couldn't believe all of the propaganda around that and how we were set up as American citizens to be for or against America! So many of us didn't want a war, but a lot of artists were being told to be silent. I was a new artist and I was an independent artist, so I felt like I could pretty much say what I wanted to say even though it might affect my future in a bad way. I can just hope that it doesn't!

This is my opportunity to introduce who I am before someone tells me to be quiet. I don't think that any of the songs I do are just considered political, because I like them all to be personal.

Right now I am recording a lot of love songs and I am also recording songs that I feel reflect the censorship and co-optation of a lot of the ways artists used to be able to express ourselves. One of the things that frustrates me right now is how many things are being taken away from people and children, specifically art and music. Meanwhile, we are being told that we're being protected right now and that it is in our best interest. It is a very weird time.

A few months ago, when I first started recording my new album, the songs I was writing were more about my frustrations with the times. More recently, it's been more love songs. I am just open to all of the creative energy. The last presidential election [in 2004] pushed me to want to keep on moving and not get caught up in feeling hopeless.

**JM:** Many musicians and artists have spoken out against the war in Iraq and some, like the Dixie Chicks for example, were attacked for speaking out. Tell me more about what you were doing in your musical career at that time and how you felt about seeing that happen.

**GM:** I am twenty-seven years old now and I feel that I am witnessing a time that I have never witnessed before. My mother, who was alive in the fifties and sixties, said that it was a similar climate of fear and repression. You know, if you say certain things or if you don't look like you're patriotic, you are in danger and you could be ostracized. As musicians, we have such an opportunity to express how we feel and how so many people feel. I really appreciated seeing different artists come out and say, "I am not for this war."

I was surprised and disappointed when I heard that even at awards shows, people's microphones were going to be turned off or they weren't going to be invited to the next awards show if they spoke up and said something. Are we back to the fifties before the Civil Rights movement? Are we just supposed to go along with the flow and nobody can say anything?

I personally feel like I had a little bit more freedom as such a new artist and an independent artist. I could pretty much say what I wanted to say, but I was also nervous. I don't feel that everyone was united before and everyone was treated equally before the September 11th attacks. So afterward, when everyone was supposed to not say anything and unite to fight for freedom, it was very confusing. And we are supposedly bringing freedom to other people by killing! The whole thing is just so crazy. I think that for so many of us it was obvious that the war in Iraq was also about money. It seems as though people who are not generally antiwar would know this war is being fought for the wrong reasons.

**JM:** You told me that when you perform you speak about these issues in between songs.

**GM:** Yeah, sometimes. Most of my songs are love songs. It really depends on what night you come to a show because I am either really talkative on stage or I'm really quiet and just focused on the music. It really depends on how engaged people are and what they feel like hearing or what I feel like I need to say that other people aren't saying.

JM: You mentioned that some of your family is Jewish and your father is from South Africa. Both sides of your family have experienced a lot of suffering, in Germany during the Holocaust and in South Africa during apartheid.

I know that you have been to South Africa. I wonder what you can say about your visits there and also how the history of your family has affected you and your ideas about social change, and how that has come into your music.

GM: A heavy question! I have family still in South Africa and family still in Germany, German Jews. My great-grandmother didn't make it through the Holocaust, but my grandmother left in time. And I was born in Oakland, California, and have lived only in America.

In my South African grandfather's lifetime, he saw the whole shift of power and economically things being crazy and was forcibly moved to different neighborhoods. I can't afford to forget. I can't afford to not be thankful. I can't afford to not take advantage of saying what I need to say. I don't feel so far removed from their oppression. I know the history of this country. From the Native American genocide to slavery, a lot of people's families in this country have been through a lot.

JM: My sense is that some of the great social change movements have had some basis in spiritual transformation. I think of Martin Luther King, Jr., and Mohandas Gandhi and Malcolm X after his visit to Mecca. What is your view about the relationship between social change and spiritual or personal transformation?

GM: A lot of leaders have had that spiritual connection. Not everybody talks about it. Political leaders risk their lives and they could die any day. Their families are often in danger because of what they're saying, so I think it's important to be connected to something much larger then yourself.

As for me, what is my spiritual connection? I am still figuring it out. I wasn't raised religiously. I have always valued spirituality and I believe that what you put out into the world comes back. I am not identified with a certain religion, but I definitely have a spirituality and I think it's really important to keep focused on how we are all connected.

JM: Martin Luther King, Jr., said, "We are all inextricably linked in a web of mutuality." Why would I ever want to do you harm—you are a part of me. Your song "Salvation" has that same kind of compassion. You sing on it, "I can feel the pain of the world" and "I pray to an unknown God, please reveal yourself to me." I hear a real longing to be in touch with that connection and also feeling how those who are suffering feel.

GM: It is really interesting, because the way my name was written cursive on the CD cover, some people thought it said "gospel." Especially when they saw that one of the song titles was "Salvation!" I love gospel music, probably because of the feeling. "Salvation" was one of those songs where this chorus just came to me on and on and finally I was able to shape it into a song.

JM: In the song "Catch 22," you sing about the suffering that comes from jealousy and indecision. Do you have anything to offer about what you have learned about relaxing fear and confusion and being open to change?

GM: I know that when I am scared of things, it can block my forward movement so much. It is incredible and devastating. That is what oppression can do. It can make you think, "You are never going to be able to do this" or "How dare you think that you can do anything you want in this world?" and "What are your resources?" "What class are you in?" and "What can you afford?"

JM: Do you mean that when people are told these things, they then tell themselves these negative messages?

GM: Definitely. I fight those kinds of thoughts all the time. I think that, for one, my mother has raised me to think that whatever I truly want to do, I can do it, if I put the effort in. She has encouraged me in the things that I love to do. And I am part of this organization for women and girls, Be Present, that creates peer-led support groups to talk about our fears and our goals and figure out how to move forward and not let distress stop us and get in the way. I am so thankful that I have had these positive messages since I was young, because I can tell now, when I don't want to do something or when something can be undermined, I can tell that it is just my fear. I might be scared of the outcome, afraid of both failure and success. I could try my hardest and get an incredible response or I could try my hardest and fail.

When I was younger, I tried only so hard. And it could pass, and it could still be impressive, but I would know that I wasn't giving up everything. As I have let go of some of my fears, I've decided that I am just going to put it all out there the best that I can, and let things keep growing. I can keep making higher goals. I have put it out there and I am just going to get over what the outcome is. I will just dream of what I want the outcome to be and sometimes that's what it ends up being.

When I was finishing the first album, I was proud of it and I was so critical of it. There was so much more that I wanted to do and it was really hard for me and I just said, "This is it. I am just going to let it go and it is going to be what it is." That's what it is about!

JM: How important do you think nonviolence is in terms of social change? Is that something that you view as an important component of making positive social change?

GM: I think that communication is really important. And organizing. Yes. I will be very happy if things can be solved, and if we can really be in a better place with nonviolence. I feel like that is always a better way. I don't know what it's going to take to feel like there is actually a sense of equality in the United States. I really wonder what that's going to take.

JM: I have the idea that it is an ongoing process. Though we may never arrive at a point of complete equality, we can aim towards it.

GM: I think the first step is all of us opening our eyes to what is actually happening in the world before it is too late. This is really important.

JM: What do you see when your eyes are open? I think of your song "It Takes More," about a fourteen-year-old boy and the experiences he's had in his life—being told he'd never amount to anything, being beaten by his father, and ending up in prison.

GM: I think there is definitely racism in the court system. I think it is sad that a lot of money is going toward building youth prisons and jails. People, mostly black males, are being locked away for things that I don't think they need to be locked away for. That is one of the saddest things I can think of. A lot of the other issues are economic, such as fewer people being able to afford health care, childcare being less available or too expensive, art and music classes being cut in schools. Those things affect so many young people's lives.

JM: A writer at *Rolling Stone* magazine included you in a list of ten artists to keep an eye on. I imagine that that feels exciting and possibly also disconcerting, that maybe you have an image to live up to.

GM: It was really exciting for me. It happened at the same time that I opened for the MTV2 Sisters of Soul Concert. And we were independent at the time and I just felt really lucky to be mentioned. I was an independent artist getting some national attention from a known publication. It just felt like something big, some recognition. And I felt like it was going to open some doors nationally. That's how I felt. It was pretty exciting and made me want to work harder.

JM: These days you're working on a new album. What can you tell me about this new work?

GM: It is a little different musically just because I am learning more all the time. Just even in my writing. The musicians and producers I am working with are also growing. I feel very proud of what we're creating.

I am also just trying to have fun with this album and explore different parts of myself and not be limited creatively. *Even Closer* was pretty eclectic also, but this time I am trying to go to all the extremes and just go with what I am feeling. I think that's what I have appreciated about a lot of other artists who I admire. Stevie Wonder and "Happy Birthday" to Martin Luther King, Jr. as a way to talk about how he should be recognized with a national holiday. It might not sound like a political song, but it had a huge political impact. I am doing it all right now.

JM: You mentioned "Red, White, and Blues" from the *Even Closer* album. Are there songs on this new album that are more political or more directly about social issues?

GM: There is this song, "Change It All," about small businesses, schools, and libraries closing and the giant stores that are popping up everywhere. It is a mellow track with the words: "I have been waiting restlessly for the words to a song that could change it all."

JM: A lot of people have that same feeling now. And together, I hope, we'll carry that through.

# Goapele Mohlabane Selected Discography

*Closer* – 2001 (Skyblaze Recordings)
*Even Closer* – 2002/2004 (Red Urban Records/Skyblaze Recordings)

# ACKNOWLEDGMENTS

MY GRATITUDE to all of my family, friends, and mentors who have encouraged and supported my work over the years. My appreciation to Rachel, Travis, Martha, Heidi, Terry, Sarah, and Sophie at Parallax Press. Special thanks to Rachel for her suggestion that this book be a compilation of interviews with musicians and that it include a CD.

My deep thanks go to all of the musicians who took the time and energy to speak with me, and to all those who helped coordinate and set up the interviews, including publicists, assistants, managers, producers, venue owners, and record labels.

My parents, Bill and Bernice Malkin, shared sympathetic joy with me throughout the creation of this book. Thanks to Alison Richards for your love and empathy.

Thanks to Bruneau Babet for generously offering me the use of a laptop computer for this and other writing projects and to Gabriel Constans for encouraging me to have my work published.

Thich Nhat Hanh has been an inspiration and source of peace for me for many years and I am particularly grateful to have his words for the foreword to *Sounds of Freedom*. Thank you also to all the teachers who have pointed me in a helpful direction, including Mary Orr and Richard Shankman of Vipassana Santa Cruz, Jean Morrison and Christine King of the Santa Cruz Center for Compassion, and Bob Stahl of the mindfulness-based Stress Reduction Program.

I extend my gratitude to the listeners and supporters of Free Radio Santa Cruz, a commercial-free, collectively-run, micro-broadcast radio station that has been operating since 1995 without a license from the US government. Special thanks to all those who helped to establish the station and keep it running and to those who have contributed their voices: Skidmark Bob, Vinny Lombardo, George, Uncle Dennis, Phil Free, Ann, Robert Norse,

Hobo Lee, Matthew, Jason, Aeon Blues, C-Line, Amy, Cassandra, Matt, Bill, Evelyn, Louie, R-Duck, Earth Mommer, Romedo, Reckless, Mistress Violet, Damian, Javier, Max, Durt, Danielsan, Joser, Payaso, Bradley, Emily, Sandino, Kim Argula, Ed Frey, Becky and Rachel Johnson, Worker Will, DJ Suzie, Tom Schriener, Spirit, Jen, Sista Snatch, Manifesto, Sandy Roth, Puck, and Merlin. Listen on the internet at www.freakradio.org!

PARALLAX PRESS, a nonprofit organization, wishes to deeply thank the following gracious donors for helping to make this publication a reality:

Mary Hillebrand & Angie Hickerson

Marion & Allan Hunt-Badiner

Don Katz

Mark Nguyen

Shane Snowdon

Doris Wheeler

Parallax Press publishes books on engaged Buddhism and the practice of mindfulness by Thich Nhat Hanh and other authors. As a division of the Unified Buddhist Church, we are committed to making these teachings accessible to everyone and preserving them for future generations. We believe that, in doing so, we help alleviate suffering and create a more peaceful world. All of Thich Nhat Hanh's work is available at our on-line store and in our free catalog. For a copy of the catalog, please contact:

Parallax Press
P.O. Box 7355
Berkeley, CA 94707
www.parallax.org
Tel: (510) 525-0101

Monastics and laypeople practice the art of mindful living in the tradition of Thich Nhat Hanh at retreat communities in France and the United States. Individuals, couples, and families are invited to join these communities for a Day of Mindfulness and longer practice periods. For information, please visit www.plumvillage.org or contact:

Plum Village
13 Martineau
33580 Dieulivol, France
info@plumvillage.org

Green Mountain Dharma Center
P.O. Box 182
Hartland Four Corners, VT 05049
mfmaster@vermontel.net
Tel: (802) 436-1103

Deer Park Monastery
2499 Melru Lane
Escondido, CA 92026
deerpark@plumvillage.org
Tel: (760) 291-1003

For a worldwide directory of Sanghas practicing in the tradition
of Thich Nhat Hanh, please visit www.iamhome.org.

green press
INITIATIVE

# SOUNDS OF FREEDOM
## COMPILATION CD CREDITS

"Incense Offering" by Thich Nhat Hanh. From *Chanting Breath by Breath*, courtesy of Unified Buddhist Church, Inc. Copyright 2002.

"Evolve" by Ani DiFranco. From *Evolve*, courtesy of Righteous Babe Music/BMI. Copyright 2003.

"Tell Somebody (Repeal the Patriot Act)" by Rickie Lee Jones. From *The Evening of My Best Day*, courtesy of Rickie Lee Jones and V2 Records. Copyright 2003.

"Closer" by Goapele. From *Even Closer*, courtesy of Skyblaze Recordings. Copyright 2002.

"Putting a Face on God" by John Trudell. From *Trudell Truths*, courtesy of Daemon Records. Copyright 2002.

"Forgive to Forget" by Michelle Shocked. Courtesy of Michelle Shocked/Mighty Sound. Copyright 2002.

"Heven Tonite" by Boots Riley, performed by The Coup. From *Party Music*, courtesy of Boots Riley/75 Ark. Copyright 2001.

"Perfect World" by Indigo Girls. From *All That We Let In*, courtesy of Sony/Epic Records. Copyright 2004.

"Statue of Liberty" by Laurie Anderson. From *Life on A String*, courtesy of Nonesuch Records. Copyright 2001.